GABRIELLE CHANEL

With the support of

CHANEL

In partnership with

First published by V&A Publishing to accompany the exhibition *Gabrielle Chanel. Fashion Manifesto*, on view from 16 September 2023 to 25 February 2024 at the Victoria and Albert Museum, South Kensington, London SW7 2RL

Distributed in North America by Abrams, an imprint of ABRAMS

ISBN: 978 1 83851 039 8 (Hardback)
ISBN: 978 1 83851 044 2 (Paperback)

10 9 8 7 6 5 4 3 2 1
2027 2026 2025 2024 2023

A catalogue record for this book is available from the British Library.

Designer: Daniela Rocha
Copy-editor: Linda Schofield
Indexer: Nic Nicholas
Colour origination: DL Imaging
New photography: Nicholas Alan Cope

Printed by Graphius, Belgium

Back cover illustration: detail of fig.1
p.4: detail of no.28
p.6: detail of no.3
p.8: detail of no.19
p.288: detail of no.62

V&A Publishing

Supporting the world's leading museum of art and design, the Victoria and Albert Museum, London

GABRIELLE CHANEL

EDITED BY
ORIOLE CULLEN & CONNIE KAROL BURKS

WITH NEW PHOTOGRAPHY BY
NICHOLAS ALAN COPE

V&A PUBLISHING

CONTENTS

FOREWORD

Tristram Hunt
Director, V&A

Gabrielle Chanel was a master of her art. Her incredible output, from a career spanning more than six decades, paved the way for the contemporary wardrobes we recognize today. As one of the most successful fashion houses in existence, Chanel owes much to the templates first laid down over a century ago by its founder, Gabrielle Chanel.

Gabrielle Chanel. Fashion Manifesto charts the evolution of Chanel's iconic design style from the opening of her first millinery boutique in Paris in 1910 to the showing of her final collection in 1971. Drawing upon the exhibition *Gabrielle Chanel. Manifeste de mode* – organized by the Palais Galliera, Fashion Museum of the City of Paris – it is an honour to present this exhibition reimagined by the Victoria and Albert Museum. We are enormously grateful for the support of Chanel and to work in partnership with the Palais Galliera. I extend my thanks to Bruno Pavlovksy, president of Chanel SAS and president of Chanel Fashion; Hélène Fulgence, director of the Patrimoine de CHANEL; and to the original curators, Miren Arzalluz, director of the Palais Galliera, and Véronique Belloir, head of collections at the Palais Galliera.

As the designated National Collection of Fashion, the V&A holds one of the largest and most important collections of dress and textiles in the world. *Gabrielle Chanel. Fashion Manifesto* utilizes the V&A's exceptional twentieth-century couture, while also drawing on objects from the Theatre and Performance, Prints and Drawings, Photography, Archives, and Jewellery collections, which come together to tell a rich story of design ambition, innovation and creativity.

The exhibition, and this accompanying publication – with fantastic new photography by Nicholas Alan Cope – places a spotlight on the little-known Chanel garments within the V&A's collection and presents them alongside incredible works from the Patrimoine de CHANEL and the Palais Galliera. It also draws on unique Chanel garments from other collections around the world and closer to home, including some spectacular early dresses from Pickford's House, Derby Museums.

Gabrielle Chanel. Fashion Manifesto builds on the V&A's world-renowned fashion exhibition programme: from the record-breaking *Christian Dior: Designer of Dreams* to the paradigm-shifting *Alexander McQueen: Savage Beauty* and agenda-setting *Fashioned from Nature*. With *Gabrielle Chanel. Fashion Manifesto* – the first UK show dedicated to the supremely inventive designer – the trajectory of pioneering fashion exhibitions continues at the V&A.

Miren Arzalluz
Director, Palais Galliera

*One world was ending, another was about to be born. I was in the right place;
an opportunity beckoned, I took it […] What were needed were simplicity, comfort
and neatness: unwittingly, I offered all of that.*

Gabrielle Chanel

On 1 October 2020 the Palais Galliera, Fashion Museum of the City of Paris, presented *Gabrielle Chanel. Manifeste de Mode*, the first retrospective ever dedicated to the French couturière in Paris. This ambitious project was also the inaugural exhibition of a renovated and extended Palais Galliera, which included the newly created Galeries Gabrielle Chanel.

Gabrielle Chanel. Manifeste de Mode explored the long career of the trailblazing designer that altered the course of fashion twice in her lifetime: during her early years as a game-changing designer in the 1910s, and once again after her unexpected and extraordinary return to fashion in 1954. The exhibition focused on the aesthetic and technical characteristics of her work and the emergence and development of her legendary style, her own radical manifesto that has influenced fashion to this day. After a memorable success in Paris, we presented the exhibition at the exceptional international venues the National Gallery of Victoria in Melbourne (5 December 2021 – 25 April 2022) and the Mitsubishi Ichigokan Museum in Tokyo (18 June – 25 September 2022), reaching, and engaging with, new and diverse audiences.

Today, we are honoured to have a new and reimagined chapter of this challenging project, presented at the Victoria and Albert Museum in London. On behalf of Paris Musées and the Palais Galliera, I would like to sincerely thank Tristram Hunt, director of the V&A, and Daniel Slater, director of exhibitions at the V&A, for this most fruitful and stimulating partnership. I would equally like to extend my thanks to Oriole Cullen, senior curator of Fashion and Textiles at the V&A, for her excellent and rigorous work, as well as project curators Connie Karol Burks and Stephanie Wood. Oriole has worked in close collaboration with Hélène Fulgence and the formidable team at Patrimoine de CHANEL, as well as with Véronique Belloir, head of collections at the Palais Galliera, and with whom I had the immense pleasure of curating *Gabrielle Chanel. Manifeste de Mode*. My heartfelt thanks and appreciation also go to our colleagues at the Paris Musées and Palais Galliera who worked with passion and dedication to make this exhibition possible.

The Palais Galliera is most grateful for the unconditional support of Chanel from the inception of this project. I would like to express my gratitude to Bruno Pavlovsky, president of Chanel SAS and president of Chanel Fashion, and Laurence Delamare, director of 7L and director of fashion editorial at Chanel, for their support as well as for their unwavering commitment to the conservation and enhancement of fashion heritage.

INTRODUCTION

Oriole Cullen &
Connie Karol Burks

Gabrielle Chanel's undeniable impact on women's wardrobes – during her lifetime and beyond – distinguishes her as one of the most influential figures of twentieth-century western fashion. Along with Chanel's professional oeuvre, her long and complex private life has also been, in turns, a focus of fascination, admiration, condemnation and intrigue. As a figure she has prompted countless biographies that delve into far more detail than this brief account can encompass.[1] On the subject of her own life, Chanel is an unreliable narrator. She mythologized much of her past, obscuring certain elements and fabricating others, making her biography a complicated and often contradictory story for scholars and commentators to unravel. She was undeniably shaped by the hardship of her early years and the social constraints of the period, which left her with a determination to succeed at any cost.

This window onto the life and work of Chanel is framed by the clothes and accessories that she designed: a selection of key garments is explored in detail in the gallery of photographs that follows this introduction. Her incredible output was so directly shaped by her own experiences, desires and interests that the surviving gowns, suits and scents which she created each give a particular insight into her extraordinary life.

CHILDHOOD

Gabrielle Chanel was born in Saumur, France, on 19 August 1883. Her father, Albert Chanel, an impoverished travelling salesman, married her mother, Jeanne Devolle, the following year. The growing family lived in poverty, with Jeanne and the children sometimes accompanying Albert on the road. When Jeanne died in 1895, Chanel and her two sisters went to live in a Catholic orphanage in Aubazine. Her two younger brothers were taken in as farmhands by local families. At 18, Chanel enrolled as a charity student at Notre Dame boarding school in Moulins, where she did housework in return for schooling and accommodation. It was here that she honed the needlework skills first learnt at the orphanage.

On leaving the school, she worked alongside her aunt Adrienne (who was a year older) as a seamstress for a tailor and as a sales assistant in À Sainte-Marie, a lingerie and hosiery boutique in Moulins. Adrienne and Gabrielle began to enjoy their independence, visiting the town's cabarets and eventually becoming regular performers on stage at the music café La Rotonde, which was popular with local soldiers. Here, Gabrielle caught the eye of the textile heir Étienne Balsan. In around 1906 Chanel moved to Vichy and worked at the Théâtre de l'Alcazar and music hall before joining Balsan on his estate at Royallieu. Chanel lived a life of leisure: reading, horse riding and mingling with Balsan's eclectic set (see fig.2). It was during this time that she first met Arthur 'Boy' Capel, a wealthy

Fig. 1 Gabrielle Chanel, *c.*1932. Photograph by Curtis Moffat. V&A: E.298–2009, given by Penelope Smail

Fig. 2 Gabrielle Chanel, Léon de
Laborde and Étienne Balsan in
front of the stables at Royallieu,
*c.*1909. Private collection

Fig. 3 Gabrielle Chanel and her
aunt Adrienne Chanel, Vichy,
1906. Private collection

Fig. 4 Portrait of Gabrielle
Chanel, 1909

English businessman who she later described as 'the only man I have
loved'.[2] She remained at Balsan's chateau for a couple of years, after which
time she became interested in her own venture, designing and making
women's hats. She began selling these to Balsan's affluent friends, including
his ex-mistress Émilienne d'Alençon, a dancer, actor and courtesan who
moved in fashionable circles.

A BEGINNING IN MILLINERY

In 1909 Gabrielle Chanel moved to Paris to officially establish her business,
a millinery salon at 160 boulevard Malesherbes in an apartment lent to her
by Balsan.

 While fellow couturiers Jeanne Lanvin and Madame Grès also
began their careers in millinery, they had trained within the industry.
Chanel had a good eye and was a strong stylist, but aware of her lack
of technical expertise, she recruited Lucienne Rabaté, a highly skilled
milliner from the fashionable millinery House of Maison Lewis who
brought a loyal clientele with her.[3] Chanel's younger sister Antoinette

Fig. 5 Hats by Gabrielle Chanel modelled by herself, *Comoedia illustré*, 1 October 1910

joined her as an assistant. Owing to the great success of the venture and with the encouragement and backing of Boy Capel, 1910 saw the opening of Chanel's first boutique, Chanel Modes, at 21 rue Cambon. In October of that year the designer appeared in the fashion and theatre magazine *Comoedia illustré* with a feature depicting her modelling her own hats (fig.5).

In the first decade of the twentieth century, the hat played a crucial role as a fashion signifier, an instantly visible sartorial statement. Chanel's rejection of the excessively feminine fashions of the Belle Époque was markedly noticeable in her own choice of headwear. It was the simplified unadorned hats that she wore in her everyday life, a part of her own unique style, that had initially sparked interest among the fashionable racing crowd with whom she socialized: for example, the lacquered straw boater, decorated with ribbon and a spotted veil, in which Chanel was photographed at a racecourse in 1907 (fig.6), or the unique soft round-crowned 'flattened melon', an unstructured version of the bowler hat, that she chose to wear on horseback.[4] The hats offered at Chanel Modes were stripped-back versions of the excessively large accessories dramatically piled with silk flowers or feathers that still dominated fashion at the time. Although Chanel's early creations adhered to general fashionable silhouettes and often incorporated substantial feather decorations, her hats were less fussy, with a more masculine style (see no.1). Often designed to be worn at an angle, they made a strong graphic statement.

Fig. 6 Gabrielle Chanel at a racecourse in the south of France, 1907. Private collection

Fig. 7 Gabrielle Chanel and
Arthur 'Boy' Capel, *Tangoville-sur-Mer*, 1913. Illustration by Sem.
V&A: 225–1953

Fig. 8 Gabrielle Dorziat in costume
for *Le Diable Ermite*, wearing a hat by
Gabrielle Chanel, *Comoedia illustré*,
20 November 1912

Chanel's hats were publicized on and off stage by actresses including her friend Gabrielle Dorziat, as well as Lucienne Roger and Geneviève Vix, who all appeared modelling her creations in magazines like *Comoedia illustré* and *Les Modes* (fig.8). Dorziat wore Chanel's work on stage in productions such as *Bel Ami* and *Le Diable Ermite*.[5]

Chanel herself was conscious of the value of promoting her own image as part of the publicity for her business. The caricaturist Sem (Georges Goursat, 1863–1934) published several drawings of Chanel, the first in 1913 in his satirical book *Tangoville-sur-Mer*,[6] which parodied the fashionable crowd at Deauville. Depicted as a centaur, Boy Capel sweeps Chanel the milliner off her feet, her hatbox flying out before her (fig.7). On the end of his polo mallet Capel balances a hat. Although not particularly flattering, this caricature is a testament to the fact that Chanel was now a recognizable figure in fashionable society.

EXPANSION AND JERSEY

Throughout her career Chanel was inspired by the simplicity and practicality of menswear and sporting clothes. She created her first garments primarily from jersey, which was largely the preserve of men's sporting shirts and underwear.[7] With properties of fit and stretch, jersey offered a departure from the stiff tailoring and constricting bodices and dresses found in fashionable women's wardrobes of the early twentieth century. More radically, it was an inexpensive utilitarian textile, a world away from the luxurious materials associated with haute couture. Chanel's name soon became synonymous with this fabric, with *Vogue* noting that 'Chanel is master of her art and her art resides in jersey'.[8] A very early Chanel garment was a belted sweater with dropped shoulders and a deep V-neck (fig.9). Made with undyed wool jersey supplied by the firm of Rodier, it was described by Chanel biographer Edmonde Charles-Roux as 'reminiscent in form of the sailor blouse and in fabric of the jockey's pullover',[9] and referred to in *Vogue* in 1914 as 'the middy sweater in fine jersey that was so successfully launched by Gabrielle Chanel last year'.[10] As her style evolved, Chanel often mixed different gauges of jersey together in her suits: for example, a silk jersey for the top (see no.2) and a more robust wool jersey for the skirt.[11]

In 1912, following the success of her Parisian millinery establishment, Chanel expanded her business, choosing the town of Deauville as the site of her new venture. This smart seaside resort, with a racetrack and casino, frequented by Parisian and international high society, presented an opportunity to capture the summer trade following the seasonal exodus from the city. It was well known in fashionable circles that 'at Deauville one can get a birds-eye view of the new fashions'.[12] In Paris, Chanel was permitted to sell only millinery at 21 rue Cambon. This was due to the presence of another dressmaker and a related clause in the lease. The new Deauville boutique offered her the perfect opportunity to trial a collection of clothing alongside her hats.[13]

Situated at the centre of Deauville on the bustling rue Gontaut-Biron, a popular thoroughfare 'along which, from eleven to one each day, Deauville sits and walks and observes itself critically',[14] Chanel's boutique was perfectly placed to draw a fashionable crowd. Her garments were ideal for an informal seaside wardrobe and were an instant success that showed no sign of abating. As *Vogue* noted, 'to look once at a Chanel jersey costume is to desire it ardently'.[15]

The outbreak of war in 1914 did little to dent the Chanel business: to serve the city dwellers who had retreated to the coast she ensured that her Deauville premises remained open. Keen to expand her business further, in 1915 Chanel decided to repeat her coastal experiment and cement her place in fashion by opening her first couture house in the internationally fashionable resort of Biarritz in the Villa Larralde on rue Gardères. The

Fig. 9 Gabrielle Chanel on the
beach at Étretat, 1913

southerly location of Biarritz on the border between France and Spain
meant a much longer season and a stream of wealthy clients from neutral
Spain with whom Chanel was more than ready to engage. Noted as a hive
of sporting activity and outdoor pursuits, Biarritz was the perfect location
for Chanel. She had by this time become celebrated for her sportswear,[16]
with her loose-fitting coats and relaxed jersey sweaters suitable for golf,
tennis and seaside exercise. The casinos and smart hotels also demanded
stylish eveningwear, which Chanel was well situated to provide.

As the First World War moved towards its end, Chanel's business
continued to prosper. In 1918 she opened her Paris couture house at
31 rue Cambon, taking over the entire building. This enabled her to
consolidate the salons, her creative studio and the workrooms all in one
place, with a small apartment on the second floor. From the beginning of
the 1920s there was additionally a boutique on the ground floor. Within
the next decade as her empire grew further, Chanel came to occupy five
buildings in the street.

BLACK DRESS

By 1919 life in Paris had sprung back to a frenetic pace in the aftermath of
the war. In January of that year, the Peace Conference brought an influx
of international delegations to the city. Yet disruptions and shortages were
still part of everyday living. Commenting on issues such as a lack of transport
and the curtailed resources of many clients, *Vogue* noted that Chanel had taken
these considerations on board when designing her latest collection, 'thus Mlle
Chanel has confined herself almost entirely to black costumes for evening
wear, and these items are short and round of corsage, so that they might
even be worn in the afternoon under a long manteau'.[17] This acknowledged
the altering attitudes towards the traditional custom of changing clothes at
set times throughout the day. While ostensibly Chanel's black dresses were a
practical seasonal decision, she was alert to the invaluable flexibility of black
garments and how they could be an essential component in her proposition
for the modern wardrobe. She later claimed that it was a purely aesthetic
decision. In various differing accounts she said the inspiration had come to
her one evening as a result of seeing her contemporaries dressed up in
fashionable colours of the time, which she abhorred, and she was hit with
the realization that the women 'ought to be dressed in black'.[18]

Some conjectured that Chanel had popularized black, traditionally a
colour of mourning, due to the death of her beloved Boy Capel in a car crash
in December 1919. Although he had recently married, they had continued
their affair and his loss devastated her. However, she refuted this claim, telling
biographer Marcel Haedrich that it was a scurrilous rumour started by Elsa
Maxwell in her newspaper column, who speculated that the unmarried

Chanel could not publicly mourn Capel and so decided to force everyone into black. Chanel said she found Maxwell's comments in 'bad taste'.[19]

Although Chanel was certainly not the only designer to use black, it was a colour with which she became inextricably linked, most specifically in relation to a crepe de Chine day dress of 1926, model 817 (fig.10). A simple long-sleeved, knee-length dress, it was decorated with a series of crossing pintucks, a signature detail that Chanel incorporated into numerous day dresses of the period in fabrics including jersey and raw silk. *Vogue* predicted it was 'the frock that all the world will wear',[20] and likened it to the 15 million black Model T cars sold by Henry Ford. The black dress remained a staple in Chanel's collections, in fabrics from crepes and chiffons to jerseys and satins. The colour also served as a perfect ground for eye-catching embellishment.

EMBROIDERY

The early 1920s saw Chanel experiment with different styles of decoration and embroidery. Some of Chanel's most noteworthy embroideries of this period were executed by the House of Kitmir (see nos 9 and 10), established in around 1922 by the Russian Grand Duchess Maria Pavlovna Romanova (1890–1958) (fig.11). Pavlovna was one of many Russian aristocrats who had fled Russia following the Revolution of 1917. Chanel had met Duchess Pavlovna through her brother, Grand Duke Dmitri Pavlovich (1891–1942), who was residing in France at the time. Pavlovich had been exiled from Russia in 1917 for his part in the assassination of Rasputin. The Grand Duke and Duchess were grandchildren of Tsar Alexander II and much of their family was executed during the Revolution. While the siblings had lost the wealth and splendour to which they were accustomed, their social standing and connections in France were intact.

According to Pavlovich's diary, he first met Chanel in Paris in 1911 and this acquaintance was re-established when the pair met again through mutual friends in 1920 in Biarritz. As later recounted to Paul Morand, Chanel was 'captivated' by Pavlovich and his circle but at the time was still romantically involved with the composer Igor Stravinsky.[21] In 1921, however, she had begun a romantic relationship with Pavlovich that lasted about a year, thereafter transforming into a long-term friendship. His cousin-in-law would model in Chanel's 1932 London dress show (see p.32). Chanel later described herself as 'fascinated' by the Russian émigrés in her social circle and this interest manifested in her designs of the period.[22] As noted in *Vogue*, Chanel employed several Russian émigrés at her salon.[23] These influences seen in both her professional and personal lives have led some biographers and fashion historians to refer to the early 1920s as Chanel's 'Slavic period'.[24]

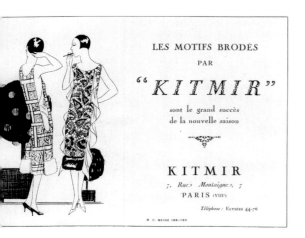

LES MOTIFS BRODÉS
PAR

" *KITMIR* "

sont le grand succès
de la nouvelle saison

KITMIR
7, Rue Montaigne, 7
PARIS (VIIIᵉ)

Téléphone : ELYSÉES 44-76

R. C. SEINE 189-130

Fig. 12 Chanel N°5, 1927.
Illustration by Sem

PERFUME

The beginnings of what later became one of the world's most recognized and celebrated perfumes emerged in 1920 when Chanel was introduced to Ernest Beaux, the man who would concoct the unique and enduring fragrance. Some Chanel biographers have suggested that it was Pavlovich who made this auspicious introduction. Beaux was the former technical director for Rallet, the leading perfume and soap manufacturer in Russia, which supplied the Russian imperial court until the Revolution in 1917. Upon fleeing Russia, Beaux relocated to the south of France, where Rallet had established a perfume laboratory in Grasse, near the abundant flower fields of the area.

Soon after meeting Beaux, Chanel commissioned him to create an exceptional perfume for her couture house. Beaux had for some time been experimenting with the technique of using aldehydes in perfumes, an ingredient that stabilized and enhanced the other constituents combined with them, such as floral scents. Taking a novel approach, he used large amounts of aldehyde in the selection of sample scents he produced for Chanel, and which he identified only by number. Chanel chose sample N°5: a fragrance with a rich aroma derived from more than 80 ingredients, the most significant being Grasse jasmine, ylang-ylang, sandalwood, May rose and neroli. The use of aldehydes enabled a blended scent in which it is hard to decipher the individual components, resulting in a distinctive and, at the time, incredibly modern fragrance. Quoted a decade later, Chanel exclaimed: 'I love flowers, but I do not want to smell like a rose or a gardenia. You really should not be able to define what the delicate fragrance really is.'[25]

While N°5 was not the first perfume to use aldehydes to create a unique blended scent, it was arguably the first to introduce the technique's potential to a wide audience.[26] This, combined with clever marketing and chic packaging, enabled N°5 to set a precedent in the industry (see no.7). Initially, Chanel released N°5 gradually, relying on word-of-mouth publicity and fashion's desire for exclusivity. A 1927 illustration by Sem demonstrates the immediate demand for N°5: a fashionably dressed young woman gazes up at a bottle of the scent in apparent rapture, suggesting an intoxicating desire for the fragrance (fig.12).

Although production of N°5 at Grasse was increased, the laboratory had limited capacity. Théophile Bader, co-founder of the department store Galeries Lafayette, saw the retail potential of the scent and convinced Chanel that she needed to partner with a manufacturer and distributor large enough to meet the growing demand for her fragrances. In 1923 Bader introduced Chanel to Pierre and Paul Wertheimer, directors of the fragrance and cosmetic company Parfums Bourjois. Together, they agreed to move production of the perfumes to the Bourjois factories and in April

Fig. 13 Chanel fragrance and make-up, British *Vogue*, 28 November 1928

1924 established a new company, Les Parfums Chanel, which remained separate from Chanel's couture business. The deal apportioned Chanel 10 per cent of Les Parfums Chanel, Théophile Bader 20 per cent, with the remaining 70 per cent owned by the Wertheimer brothers. Chanel soon came to bitterly resent the terms of this arrangement, believing that her 10 per cent was unfair.

Despite this internal conflict, the perfume business thrived, particularly overseas. A reporter for the British newspaper the *Daily Mirror* wrote in 1925 that 'friends who have paid a recent visit to Paris come back raving over Chanel's perfumes'.[27] Following the triumph of N°5, Chanel released a series of successful perfumes in the subsequent years – N°22 in 1922, Gardénia in 1925, Cuir de Russie in 1927 and Bois des Îles in 1928 – although none ever gained quite the same reputation as N°5. Les Parfums Chanel also branched out into beauty products. In 1924 she created her first make-up collection, composed of lipsticks, powders and blush, and a skincare range followed in 1927 (see fig.13 and no.8). Soon, the sought-after scents and beauty products were available in retailers and department stores

Madame Gabrielle Chanel in her new apartment in the Ritz, Paris

Photo by Kollar, courtesy Harper's Bazaar

Madame Gabrielle Chanel is above all an artist in living. Her dresses, her perfumes, are created with a faultless instinct for drama. Her Perfume No. 5 is like the soft music that underlies the playing of a love scene. It kindles the imagination; indelibly fixes the scene in the memories of the players.

LES PARFUMS

CHANEL

GLAMOUR de CHANEL   GARDENIA de CHANEL   CUIR de RUSSIE (Russia Leather)

across Europe and North America. It was now possible for a much larger portion of society to own a little piece of the much-coveted Chanel name.

As the popularity of N°5 continued to grow, Chanel became increasingly frustrated by what she saw as her meagre 10 per cent share of Les Parfums Chanel. In the 1930s she engaged her lawyer Count René de Chambrun to assess her options and brought several unsuccessful lawsuits against the Wertheimers and the company in an attempt to gain control of a greater stake of the business.[28] These disputes persisted until 1947 (see p.44).

Fig. 14 Advertisement for Les Parfums Chanel, American *Harper's Bazaar*, November 1937, featuring Gabrielle Chanel in her suite at the Ritz. Photograph by François Kollar

456

Les Maisons Chanel et L. Rouff

THE RIVIERA AND *LE TRAIN BLEU*

Throughout the 1920s, the core of Chanel's company was based at her couture salon at 31 rue Cambon in Paris, although her boutiques in Deauville, Biarritz (see fig.15) and, from 1923, Cannes continued to disseminate her sought-after garments, accessories and scents.

Like other affluent Parisians, Chanel enjoyed frequent sojourns to the fashionable vacation destinations outside Paris. The tourist resorts and private chateaux of friends along the French coastlines offered all the sporting and leisure pursuits favoured by privileged members of society. In the early 1920s she spent considerable time in Biarritz, Arcachon and various spots along the south coast of France.

Chanel drew on her visits to the French Riviera when asked to design costumes for Serge Diaghilev's Ballets Russes production *Le Train Bleu* in 1924. The title of the ballet referred to the first-class train – coloured blue – that ran from Calais via Paris to the south of France, carrying wealthy individuals to the fashionable resorts. The ballet was a contemporary story, following the adventures of a group on holiday in the French Riviera, and so the costumes designed by Chanel were very much derived from

Fig. 15 Chanel's boutique in Biarritz, August 1931

Fig. 16 Lydia Sokolova, Anton Dolin, Bronislava Nijinska and Leon Woizikovsky in *Le Train Bleu* at the London Coliseum, December 1924. Photograph by Sasha. V&A: S.297–2017, Gabrielle Enthoven Collection

the leisure fashions worn by her and her circle. One of Chanel's costume designs pictured in the cast photo (fig.16), for a character based on the French tennis player Suzanne Lenglen, shows obvious similarity to a tennis dress designed by Chanel in 1927.

Chanel was one of many notable creatives involved in the production of *Le Train Bleu*. The ballet, or *opérette dansée* as Diaghilev referred to it, was based on a libretto by Jean Cocteau with a score by Darius Milhaud, and choreographed by Bronislava Nijinska. The set was by Cubist sculptor Henri Laurens, and Pablo Picasso designed the programme and theatre curtain. It was not Chanel's first foray into stage costume design. In 1922 she designed costumes for Cocteau's production of *Antigone* and worked again with him on *Orphée* in 1926, and *Les Chevaliers de la Table Ronde* and *Œdipe Roi* in 1937. She also provided single costumes as and when requested, such as one of her fashionable chiffon evening gowns for Felia Doubrovska in *Les Biches*.[29] Chanel's support of contemporary art and performance was not limited to her design input. She quietly gave financial assistance to several artists and creatives too, including Diaghilev, Cocteau and Stravinsky.[30]

It was on the Riviera that Chanel's life took another important turn when, in late 1923 in Monte Carlo, she met the 2nd Duke of Westminster, Hugh Grosvenor, for the first time, starting another relationship that proved deeply significant both personally and professionally. The pair were introduced by Vera Bate Lombardi (née Arkwright), who convinced Chanel to accept an invitation to dine on the Duke's yacht, the *Flying Cloud*. In 1928, while travelling around the area with the Duke, Chanel purchased the deeds to a property on the coast near Cannes. Here, she designed and built her villa, La Pausa, taking inspiration from the Aubazine convent of her childhood (fig.18).

Fig. 17 Gabrielle Chanel at Monte Carlo Beach, with Christian Bérard and Boris Kochno, 1932

Fig. 18 Interior view of Gabrielle Chanel's villa La Pausa in Roquebrune-Cap-Martin, French *Vogue*, May 1930. Photograph by Christian Bérard

Fig. 19 Gabrielle Chanel and Vera Bate Lombardi, *c*.1926. Collection of Edmonde Charles-Roux

TWEED

As Chanel honed her style, a recognizable innovation was her fashionable tweed sport suits. Relaxed jackets and practical skirts were twinned with complementary jersey blouses. The tweed suit for women was not her invention; a mainstay for sport and outdoor pursuits, it had been popular in women's wardrobes since the nineteenth century, particularly in Britain where it was referred to as a tailor-made. In the 1920s Chanel would be the one to make tweed fashionable, to take it from the countryside and transform it for the city. Originating in the eighteenth century in Scotland, tweed was traditionally woven from the fleece of Cheviot sheep, with colours from natural dyes, drawn from the landscape. It was a practical, warm, weighty fabric that repelled rain. Its earthy colours helped wearers blend into the scenery and it was therefore popular with those who enjoyed hunting and shooting expeditions. This included Chanel's friend Lombardi as well as Chanel herself. Due to her aristocratic family background and friendship with the Prince of Wales, Lombardi, who worked for Chanel in the 1920s as a press officer, was extremely well connected in British society. Like Chanel, she was known to adapt menswear garments for her own use (fig.19). Discussing tweed fashion in 1928, *The Graphic* magazine noted:

Fig. 20 Winston Churchill, his son
Randolph and Gabrielle Chanel at
a hunting meet near Dampierre,
northern France, 1928

The best tweed wearer of all was Miss Vera Arkwright (Mrs Bate). She was
not only the first wearer of tweeds in London but the first wearer of the
jumper we all wore for five years which was nothing else but a man's vest
with a collar put on it. She afterwards became, and still is, the foremost of
the English representatives in Paris for Chanel, and I suppose it is through
her that English clothes began to be taken seriously in Paris.[31]

Chanel's relationship with the Duke of Westminster brought her into
the centre of these British sporting pursuits, including fishing, hunting
and golf at his various estates in Cheshire, Scotland and Mimizan
in France. She came into contact with many members of the British
aristocracy such as Winston Churchill, with whom she remained lifelong
friends. Her enthusiasm for these sporting activities was remarked on by
Churchill when writing to his wife from the Duke's Scottish retreat Stack
Lodge: 'Coco is here in place of Violet [the Duke's second wife]. She
fishes from morn till night, & in 2 months has killed 50 salmon. She is
vy [very] agreeable – really a gt [great] & strong being fit to rule a man
or an Empire'.[32] In keeping with British tradition, in 1925 Chanel went
to Savile Row tailors Huntsman, to order herself several pairs of riding
breeches in twill and whipcord, and a grey riding skirt. She also ordered
a black whipcord skirt and breeches, essentially just the bottom half of a
traditional riding habit. She probably paired these with a jacket of her own
making. A 1928 photograph of Chanel attired for a hunt with Winston
Churchill and his son Randolph shows her in a classic riding skirt and
boots along with a very Chanel-style soft unstructured jacket, fastened with

Fig. 21 Ina Claire wearing a tweed outfit by Chanel, American *Vogue*, 15 November 1924. Photograph by Edward Steichen

a small leather belt around the waist (fig.20). In December 1931 Lombardi appeared in *Tatler* magazine similarly attired in classic riding skirt and breeches, with a Chanel yellow blouse, necktie and navy gaberdine jacket.

Tweed remained the British fabric of fascination for Chanel and a mainstay in her collections. She used it from the early 1920s for daywear, such as the suit of 'English herring-bone tweed in tan and white' worn by actress Ina Claire in *Vogue* in 1924 (fig.21).[33] Drawn to the natural uneven qualities of the fabric and keen to investigate the possibilities of how it could be developed, Chanel commenced a professional relationship with tweed-maker William Linton of Carlisle in the mid-1920s. With Linton she began to experiment with producing special tweeds with a soft handle that would work with her designs. In October 1927 *Vogue* reported that Chanel 'whose clothes are invariably simple, practical and beautiful, is making a feature of models of Scotch tweed in her recent collections' (no.20).[34] Chanel would later claim: 'It was me who taught the Scots how to make lightweight tweeds. I promise you I had a tough time convincing them!'[35] The reality was most likely a combination of Chanel's ideas and the weavers' expertise.

CHANEL TEXTILES

Textiles lay at the heart of Chanel's success. Her innovation in fashion owed more to her inventive way of working with fabric than in the constant reinvention of silhouette and style. It was therefore inevitable as her business grew that she would look towards the source and supply of materials. In 1926 she formed an exclusive jersey supply partnership with Aimery Blacque-Belair, the nephew of her friend Misia Sert and owner of a jersey and knit textile factory at Asnières. Chanel employed the multidisciplinary artist Ilia Zdanevich, known as Iliazd, as textile designer for this endeavour.[36] His skills ranged from an interest in structure and weaving techniques to an expertise in graphic print designs, rendering him a crucial contributor to Chanel's textile businesses. In 1928 Chanel decided to finance a new company, Tissus Chanel, incorporating Les Tricots Chanel, effectively buying out Blacque-Belair who remained as director of the company.[37] Chanel subsequently acquired a weaving mill at Maretz in northern France. In 1931 she replaced Blacque-Belair with Zdanevich to manage the Asnières factory and in 1932 he also took on the running of the Maretz business.

Despite being the owner of these textile businesses, Chanel explained that she still 'needed to find some means of extending my manufacturing capacity sufficiently to meet the growing demand, particularly for America'.[38] Impressed by the standard of the textiles she saw when attending the British Industries Fair in 1932, Chanel decided to formalize and expand her ties with the British textile industry. She already had business links and a presence in Britain, sourcing tweeds from the mid-1920s from Linton Tweeds and in 1927 opening a London couture house. Situated in one of the Duke of Westminster's Mayfair properties, French premières[39] oversaw the work of English employees at a workroom in Davies Street. The salon catered to Chanel's London clients with options such as 'a number of frocks designed for Ascot'.[40] Alongside this venture, *The Outlook* magazine, a weekly review, announced it would be publishing a series of articles by 'Chanel the great Paris couturière', dispensing advice on dress and fashion, for which they had been granted the 'World's exclusive rights' (fig.22).[41]

In 1932 Chanel established a subsidiary company, British Chanel Ltd, which acted as an umbrella under which numerous British textile manufacturers produced Chanel designs. These included voiles from Ferguson Bros Ltd, Carlisle, velvets from the Manchester Velvet Company, lace from G.W. Price, Nottingham, and wool cloth from Broadhead and Graves, Huddersfield. She hired diplomat and economist Sir Andrew McFadyean as the director for an initial term of two years, setting up headquarters at 9 South Audley Street in London. The British press reported enthusiastically on the new scheme: for each company, Chanel would 'supply designs, advice and information on weaves, texture and similar details, and they will then make the materials and market them themselves through the ordinary channels as Chanel textiles made in Great Britain. On the sales of the products Mlle Chanel will take a royalty.'[42] In fact, it was Zdanevich who designed the textiles on Chanel's behalf, accompanying the couturière on her visits to the factories.

As part of the launch, Chanel promised to show a presentation of a collection, which consisted of 130 models, 'to be open to trade buyers and the private woman will also be admitted on payment of a nominal sum, the money to be devoted to a charitable institution in which the British textile industry has an interest'.[43] Society women such as debutante Lady Pamela Smith, daughter of Lord Birkenhead, as well as Margaret, Countess de la Falaise, Deirdre Balfour and Princess Dmitri (Countess Marina Sergeievna Golenistcheva-Koutouzova) were chosen by Chanel to model the garments having been taken to Paris to be fitted for each look. The show, which opened at 39 Grosvenor Square (one of the Duke of Westminster's properties) on 6 May 1932, took place over a fortnight, with the first three days reserved for invited guests. Prince George, the Duke of Kent, attended on 6 May,[44] and the press reported excitedly on the cotton evening dresses and floral garlands used as decoration.[45] The press hailed the venture stating, 'Paris has shown us how to wear British'.[46] But the project was short-lived. The time from the genesis of the idea for British Chanel to producing the collection had been incredibly swift and soon Chanel began to realize the full implications and workload challenge of the financial and logistical commitment she had made to this stable of manufacturers. By February 1933 she had decided to abandon the British Chanel concern in favour of closer ties to one particular manufacturer and factory, similar to her arrangements in France. She wrote to McFadyean:

> No one is to blame for this. In business as in all other human activities, we must experiment in order to advance, and all experiments cannot be successful. One of the most important qualities in life is to recognise when one has made a mistake, and to correct it before it is too late, and this is what I'm anxious to do…[47]

Freed of her British Chanel obligations, Chanel immediately established a business venture with Broadhead and Graves, worsted wool manufacturers of Kirkheaton and one of the companies that had featured in the previous arrangement. With Frank Broadhead and herself listed as directors, she established Chanel Broadhead Fabrics Ltd at the end of February 1933. Chanel enlisted a third director, her nephew André Palasse, who relocated with his wife and two young

Fig. 23 Advertisement for
Ferguson Chanel fabrics,
March 1933

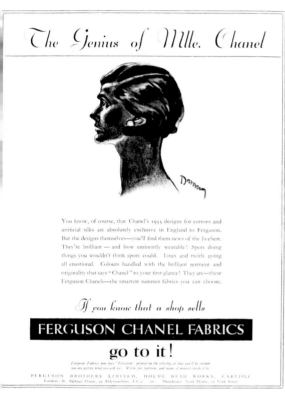

daughters to Huddersfield to oversee production at the Broadhead and
Graves factory.[48] He later moved to Lyon to manage silk production at
another factory with ties to Chanel. Broadhead and Graves enlarged
its plant and acquired new specialist machines in order to expand
the production remit from worsted for men's suiting to machine and
handwoven woollens, jersey fabrics and silks. Unlike Chanel's French
factories, situated in beautiful village settings, the mills of Yorkshire
were in more industrial environs. Chanel often visited Huddersfield,
but when she first saw the town she was reputed to have said 'comme
c'est triste' (how sad).[49]

While Chanel continued her association with other of the firms that
had been part of the earlier arrangement, they were concentrated for
sales purposes under the Chanel Broadhead name at the company's Savile
Row headquarters.[50] Chanel also collaborated with British manufacturers
to produce garments and textiles available for the general public to buy,
including knitwear from Lyle & Scott's Ellaness brand, raincoats by David
Moseley & Sons Ltd, specialists in waterproof fabrics, and a range of silk
fabrics for Harvey Nichols department store. The 1933 British Industries
Fair had a special stand dedicated to Chanel fabrics and the press noted
that when visiting the exhibition Queen Mary 'expressed interest and
pleasure in the Fergusons collaborations with Mademoiselle Chanel' and
selected for herself 'a dress length, in a quality named Fersyl in a Chanel
design' (fig.23).[51] The Duchess of York (later Queen Elizabeth and Queen
Mother) purchased a Dryart-Chanel piqué from Driver, Hartley and Co.
Ltd of Keighley.[52]

Chanel was by this time both personally and professionally involved
with the illustrator and designer Paul Iribe. He supplied designs for
Chanel's fine jewellery and textiles, as well as influencing her business
decisions. At Iribe's suggestion, Chanel had replaced Zdanevich in
1933 with his brother Dominique Iribe, who took over the running of
her French textile concerns. That same year, Iribe revived his stridently
nationalist political journal *Le Témoin*, with funding from Chanel. The
journal reflected Iribe's own xenophobic and anti-Semitic views and
included his illustrations of Marianne personifying the French nation,
which show a striking likeness to Chanel. In 1935 Iribe, who was at the
time reportedly engaged to Chanel, collapsed and died of a heart attack
while playing tennis at Chanel's villa La Pausa.

A serious recession, a knock-on effect of the Wall Street Crash, had
hit France in the early 1930s and Chanel recognized that she needed to
consolidate her businesses. In 1933 she had shut the factory at Asnières and
registered the name Tissus Chanel as a trademark. This company operated
until the outbreak of the Second World War in 1939, reviving in 1942. In
the post-war period Tissus Chanel supplied fabric to many of the top
couture houses, including Dior and Balenciaga.[53]

JEWELLERY

Chanel's influence on fashion encompassed not just garments and
scents; she also had a lasting impact on jewellery. To accompany her
sleek fashions, Chanel favoured bold and abundant jewels. Cultivating
an air of lavish nonchalance, she often paired multiple strings of pearls
or gem-encrusted chains with her simple jersey daywear (fig.24). Chanel
had amassed an impressive personal collection of fine jewellery gifted to
her over the years. However, for her clients she strongly advocated fake
gems and imitation stones and became known for popularizing costume
jewellery: in 1931 she was hailed as being 'largely responsible for the
vogue for artificial pearls'.[54] Discussing Chanel's predilection for costume
jewellery, Cecil Beaton commented that she prized jewellery 'as something
decorative or amusing, but never because it was expensive'.[55]

Chanel first began producing jewellery in around 1924. She placed her
friend Count Étienne de Beaumont (1883–1956), an aristocrat known for
his lavish fancy-dress parties and love of avant-garde art, in charge. Many
of the pieces were created by Maison Gripoix, a Parisian jewellery-maker
established in the late nineteenth century. Gripoix was known for a hand-
poured glass technique in which molten glass, under a flame, is directed
into a shaped metal setting. The metal frame is filled just enough for a
three-dimensional rounded effect. This technique allows the metal setting
to be an outline only – no back or clips are required to keep the glass in
place – resulting in a pleasing transparency and uninterrupted shapes.
Its glass paste pieces glittered almost as much as genuine precious gems.
Chanel's naturalistic floral designs of the 1930s showcased the technique to
great effect (see no.42). Gripoix also perfected a *nacrage* technique – a trade
secret – to make glass paste appear like pearls.[56]

This period marked a shift in the status of costume jewellery from being
merely an imitation of fine jewellery to being seen as a new form with
its own techniques and aesthetic.[57] Indeed, Chanel's offering of costume
jewellery was apparently no less dazzling than the real gems of royalty:
reporting on the Autumn 1927 collection, Mabel Howard of *The Sketch*
noted that 'black dresses made perfect backgrounds for the new Chanel
jewellery, lovely necklaces of crystal which reflect the rich light and shade
of the material and the surroundings' (see no.18).[58]

The Sicilian aristocrat Fulco Santostefano della Cerda, Duke of
Verdura (1898–1978), began designing jewellery for Chanel in the early
1930s. Together, Chanel and Verdura created some of the House's most
celebrated pieces. These included bold cuff bracelets encrusted with
imitation gems in rich colours, and other items inspired by Byzantine
mosaics depicting Empress Theodora. In the late 1930s Chanel also
worked with the goldsmith François Hugo (1899–1981), who designed
select jewellery pieces and possibly buttons that became a signature feature

Fig. 26 Samuel Goldwyn and Gabrielle Chanel in Los Angeles, California, 1931. Academy of Motion Picture Arts and Sciences

of her designs. Over the years, the jewellery drew inspiration from many geographies and historical epochs, often in response to Chanel's own travels abroad or the designers' visits to various museum collections.[59]

HOLLYWOOD

In February 1931 newspapers reported with great fanfare that Chanel had agreed to a deal with Hollywood film studio owner Samuel Goldwyn that would see her design the on-screen costumes and off-screen wardrobes of his United Artists studio's starlets. For the impressive fee of $1 million, Chanel travelled to Hollywood twice a year to design dresses for Goldwyn's actors, including Gloria Swanson, Ina Claire, Barbara Weeks, Charlotte Greenwood, Joan Blondell and Madge Evans. Charles-Roux reported that it was Grand Duke Dmitri who brought about the meeting of Goldwyn and Chanel while holidaying in the south of France, prompting once again a significant professional partnership for Chanel.[60]

Chanel set sail for the USA at the end of February 1931, accompanied by Misia Sert. Their arrival in New York sparked sizeable interest from American journalists, and photographs of Chanel featured widely in the press (fig.26). The event was reported enthusiastically across British papers and magazines too, with many quoting Goldwyn's promise to make Chanel the 'fashion queen of Hollywood'.[61] British periodical *The Bioscope* described Chanel as the 'famous Paris style creator' promising to 'revolutionise the gowning of stars' in Hollywood.[62]

While Chanel was already familiar with dressing Hollywood personalities off-screen and counted stars such as Ina Claire among her haute couture clients (see p.30), designing for the silver screen was a new prospect. Over the subsequent year, Chanel worked on three films for Goldwyn: *Palmy Days* (1931), *Tonight or Never* (1931; fig.27) and *The Greeks Had a Word for Them* (1932). Despite complimentary reviews of her designs and recognition that they were certainly chic, it appeared ultimately that Chanel's propositions lacked the lavish extravagance coveted by movie producers.[63] After two trips to Hollywood, Goldwyn and Chanel parted amicably, both grateful for the significant press attention each had brought the other. There was apparently no loss of face; the American magazine *Vanity Fair* acknowledged Chanel's 'laudable attempt to introduce chic to Hollywood'.[64] For Chanel, the lucrative deal had cemented her international reputation and provided valuable contacts within the American press.[65] At the end of the decade Chanel turned her hand again to film and designed the costumes for three of Jean Renoir's films, including *La Règle du Jeu* (1939).

Fig. 27 Gloria Swanson wearing
a gown designed by Gabrielle
Chanel in *Tonight or Never*, 1931.
Academy of Motion Picture Arts
and Sciences

Fig. 28 'Comet' brooch, Bijoux de
Diamants collection, Chanel, 1932.
Patrimoine de CHANEL, Paris

Fig. 29 Bijoux de Diamants
display, 1933. Sketch by Drian

BIJOUX DE DIAMANTS

A further collaboration came for Chanel in 1932, when the
International Diamond Corporation of London enlisted her to design
a range of fine jewellery comprising diamonds set in platinum. Amid
the tumultuous economic circumstances of the period following the
Wall Street Crash, the project sought to reinforce the desirability
of diamonds at a time when overt ostentation was seen by some as
abhorrent. Chanel stated that diamonds were an investment, not
an extravagance.[66] Breaking with the conventions of fine jewellery,
she presented a complete collection with unifying themes and
characteristics. Chanel's modern pieces employed a range of playful
motifs drawn from different arenas, including celestial figures of stars,
comets, the sun and moon; motifs inspired by her couture work, such
as feathers, fringes, bows and knots; and geometrical patterns (see
figs 28, 29). Janet Flanner of the *New Yorker* described them as

24 VOGUE JANVIER 1933 25

PARMI LES VISITEURS DE L'EXPOSITION CHANEL, PRINCESSE J.-L. DE FAUCIGNY-LUCINGE, MME RALLI, BARON DE GUNZBURG

BIJOUX DE DIAMANTS

DES BIJOUX POUR LA VILLE

QUELQUES PARURES EN DIAMANTS POUR LE SOIR

'dominantly and delicately astronomical'.[67] The collection included asymmetrical necklaces along with interchangeable bracelets and brooches that could also be styled as headbands or worn on hats. She used diamonds of a largely uniform size and cut, arranged in clusters, supposedly to allow their easy resetting in the future.

The public exhibition of the collection of Chanel's Bijoux de Diamants took place at her home at 29 rue du Faubourg Saint-Honoré with proceeds going to local charities.[68] The pieces were displayed on eerily lifelike wax busts, complete with made-up faces and fashionable hairstyles (fig.30). The collection gained international press attention and double-page spreads in *Vogue*. Following the exhibition, the stock of the diamond merchants De Beers reportedly jumped around 20 points on the London Stock Exchange.[69]

CONTINUED SUCCESS

The 1930s saw Chanel hailed as one of the leading names in international fashion. Both her work and her own magnetic image, which she used to promote her designs, were widely recognized and celebrated in popular society. One journalist lunching with her in 1930 commented, 'I find it truly remarkable the way in which the most sophisticated people stand or sit open-mouthed and staring at Chanel as though she were some mystery brought to life'.[70] Despite, or perhaps because of, this notoriety, within her salon Chanel preferred not to come into contact with her clients. During the showing of her collections, she hovered on her staircase, watching the room below, observing the reactions of the press and buyers reflected in the refracted mirror (fig.32). From 1935, Chanel took a suite at the Ritz, across the street from her salons on rue Cambon. While she later entertained guests at her apartment above the salons, the Ritz remained her sleeping quarters for the rest of her life.[71]

Fashion editor Diana Vreeland was a stalwart Chanel client. Reminiscing about the inter-war years she stated that a woman dressed in Chanel clothing in the 1920s and 1930s 'walked into a room and had a dignity, an authority, a thing beyond a question of taste'.[72] While Chanel had always had rivals such as Jean Patou, Edward Molyneux and Madeleine Vionnet, it was the arrival of Elsa Schiaparelli in the late 1920s that was to provide her main competition within fashionable society circles. Schiaparelli's structured tailored suits with daring Surrealist

Fig. 32 Gabrielle Chanel watching
her latest fashion presentation,
with an audience that includes
Salvador Dalí (bottom right), 1938.
Photograph by Roger Schall

embellishments offered elements of visual surprise and delight that were a
contrast to the low-key luxurious look of Chanel. Meanwhile, throughout
the 1930s Chanel continued to experiment with making her clothes as
lightweight as possible, her evening dresses consisting of the finest tulle
and lace created using intricate lingerie techniques (see nos 32 and 41). Her
advice was to 'Always dress to make yourself feel young – this means being
free and easy and unpretentious in your clothes. You have to breathe and
move and sit without being conscious of what you've got on.'[73]

SECOND WORLD WAR

> The Paris Spring season in 1939, before the war, was the gayest I had seen
> yet. There were garden parties or big cocktail parties every day and balls or
> some sort of spectacle every night for all of June and well into July.[74]

So commented American *Vogue*'s Paris correspondent Bettina Ballard when
recalling the period just before the onset of the Second World War. The
creeping inevitability of war had been hard to ignore in the final years of
the 1930s. As if in an attempt to block out the inescapable facts, fashion
had become a whirlwind of dramatic silhouettes, intensely bright colours
and intricate novelty hats.

As might be expected, Chanel called for 'lightness without frivolity',[75]
yet even her own collection for Spring/Summer 1939 shown in February
of that year was a departure from her understated looks (see no.45),
featuring 'The most romantic skirt you can manage, softly, widely full in
gypsy-stripe rayon, in parrot-coloured plaids, in chiffon or muslin voile,
in taffeta…',[76] displayed with tight bustier bodices or simple blouses and
short fitted jackets.[77] Many of the garments included a patriotic nod to the
French flag with touches of red, white and blue.

Following Adolf Hitler's invasion of Poland, on 3 September 1939
France declared war on Nazi Germany. Chanel suddenly announced that
she would be closing her couture house with immediate effect. This was
a severe blow to the thousands of employees who overnight found they
had lost their livelihoods. Many speculated that Chanel was retaliating
for labour concessions she had been forced to make to her workers three
years earlier when they had gone on strike for better working conditions.
Chanel simply stated that, 'this is no time for fashion nor for dressing the
wives of husbands who are going to be killed'.[78] Despite the efforts of
the trade union association on behalf of the workers, Chanel refused to
reconsider. Only the perfume and accessories boutique at 31 rue Cambon
remained open.[79]

In May 1940 the German army advanced into France. Anticipating
anti-Semitic violence and dispossession, Jewish brothers Paul and Pierre
Wertheimer decided to flee Paris with their families, eventually making
it to New York via South America. The brothers sold and transferred
ownership of their shares in Les Parfums Chanel to a non-Jewish business
contact, industrialist Félix Amiot.

By June 1940, Paris was under German control. The Ritz hotel,
including Chanel's suite, was requisitioned by the occupying German
officials. She, along with a few other long-term residents of the
establishment, was permitted to remain at the hotel in a smaller room.
Chanel moved the majority of her possessions into her apartment above
the haute couture salons in rue Cambon. It was during this time that she

renewed a relationship with a German embassy official, Hans Günther von Dincklage,[80] who had been exposed as a German spy in the 1936 publication *The Brown Network*.[81] Chanel's nephew André Palasse had been captured and interned as a prisoner of war in Germany. Worried for his health, Chanel appealed to Dinklage's contacts in the German authorities for Palasse's release.[82]

As part of the Nazi occupation, authorities instigated investigations into French businesses, designed to eliminate Jewish presence and transfer ownership to non-Jewish people. Inevitably, as a company publicly associated with prominent Jewish owners, an inquiry was opened into Les Parfums Chanel in January 1941. Chanel argued that, as a founder of the company, she should have indisputable priority to purchase the shares associated with the Wertheimers.[83] However, after several months of investigation, the authorities ruled that the Wertheimers' shares were now owned by Félix Amiot. He retained ownership of the shares throughout the war.[84]

While the investigation of Les Parfums Chanel was underway, in July 1941 the Nazi authorities recorded Chanel as an informant with the code name 'Westminster' and the number F7124, although it is unclear whether Chanel was ever aware of this.[85] As the code name suggests, it was her British connections that were of interest to the German authorities. This became significant in 1943. With the tide of war turning against the Nazis, Chanel and Dincklage became part of an intelligence operation that sought to use her contacts to establish a direct line of communication with British Prime Minister Winston Churchill. This plot, which became known as 'Modelhut', saw her travel to Madrid in December 1943, together with her friend and former employee Vera Bate Lombardi (see p.28), who was intimately connected to the British aristocracy and close to Churchill.[86]

When the head of the SS espionage department, Walter Schellenberg, who had sanctioned the mission, was interrogated after the war he revealed that 'Lombardi's task would be to hand over a letter written by Chanel to the British Embassy officials in Madrid for onward transmission to Churchill'.[87] However, the mission did not unfold as intended: 'instead of carrying out the part that had been assigned to her', Lombardi 'denounced all and sundry as German agents to the British authorities'. Unsurprisingly, Schellenberg assessed the mission as an 'obvious failure', adding that 'contact was immediately dropped with Chanel and Lombardi'.[88]

Just eight months later, in August 1944, Paris was liberated by the Allies. Due to her relationship with Dincklage and alleged associations with other German officials during the occupation, Chanel was arrested by the Free French Forces on suspicion of collaboration. After being detained and questioned for a few hours, she was released without charge. Chanel's activity during the war continues to cast a shadow over her legacy, and has been the subject of a large number of articles and publications over the past 70 years.

After the war, Chanel kept her couture house closed and spent much of her time in Switzerland, travelling between there, the USA, Paris and her villa in the south of France. She maintained her relationship with Dincklage for several years. Meanwhile, her legal battles over Les Parfums Chanel continued. In the summer of 1945, the Wertheimers regained control of the shares held by Amiot.[89] Paul Wertheimer died in 1947 and Pierre bought out his late brother's heirs. During this time, Chanel filed multiple lawsuits against the Wertheimers, including one in France and another in America claiming that the production of Chanel perfumes in America amounted to counterfeiting.[90] She began producing a rival perfume, under the name Mademoiselle Chanel, and sent samples to her contacts in American department stores. Pierre Wertheimer instructed his lawyers that a renegotiation was needed and, after some back and forth, the pair came to an agreement. Chanel would receive 2 per cent of all perfume sales worldwide and would maintain the right to produce Mademoiselle Chanel in Switzerland (as long as it was not called N°5). She also received an increased royalty payment on the wartime sales of Chanel perfumes, and 2 per cent royalties on all Chanel products worldwide. Finally, by the close of 1947, the company was at peace. Apparently satisfied with the deal, Chanel stopped pursuing the production of her rival perfume line in Switzerland and returned to her retirement.

Fig. 33 Allied soldiers queuing outside the Chanel boutique at 31 rue Cambon, Paris, 1945

THE RETURN

In Chanel's absence, Paris fashion was once again thriving. Many of Chanel's former competitors who had remained open throughout the war enjoyed revived success in the post-war years, including Jacques Heim, Jacques Fath, Cristóbal Balenciaga and Jean Dessès. The immediate post-war years also saw several new couture houses open and triumph, such as those of Pierre Balmain, Hubert de Givenchy and, perhaps most of all, Christian Dior. Dior's debut collection of 1947 – featuring wasp waists and scandalously voluminous skirts – caused a sensation and defined the prevailing style in Paris and beyond. What came to be known as the 'New Look' presented accentuated hourglass silhouettes created with corsets and padding that harked back to the structured S-bend styles of the Belle Époque. This hyper-feminine figure remained the ruling silhouette as the mid-1950s approached.

Meanwhile, sales of Chanel perfumes had begun to fall, possibly due to the reduced resonance of the Chanel name in the public consciousness: it was an echo of the past, a reminder of the pre-war period – the fashion world had moved on. In spring 1953 Chanel was invited by the New York perfume office to oversee the interior design of its new building.[91] Following her three-month stay in the USA, reconnecting with old acquaintances and perhaps being reminded of her previous visit while at the height of her career in 1931, Chanel made the momentous decision to revive her couture house. That year she sold the La Pausa villa and settled back permanently into her apartment above 31 rue Cambon (although continuing her habit of sleeping at the Ritz). Pierre Wertheimer agreed to pay for half of the cost of the relaunch and, re-establishing her atelier staff in the old workrooms in the same building, Chanel got back to work.[92]

Public anticipation for Chanel's return began in mid-December 1953, with the Associated Press calling it a 'bombshell for the fashion folk'.[93] American *Vogue*'s February issue featured a hyperbolic recap of Chanel's historic impact on fashion and promised detailed coverage on her return collection in the next issue.[94] On 5 February 1954 a large crowd of fashion journalists and commentators turned up to the rue Cambon salons to catch a glimpse of Chanel's first foray into fashion for 14 years. Her preceding reputation perhaps raised expectations too high: reviews were at best respectful and at worst scathing. Elizabeth Fairall in the *Washington Evening Star* reported a 'general feeling of disappointment'.[95] In Britain, the *Daily Herald* decidedly declared it a 'flop' and Geoffrey Hoare in the *Daily London News* quipped that 'the ravishing mannequins looked like little girls dressed up in their grandmother's clothes'.[96] Several commentators, however, were not so quick to disregard Chanel's return. British journalist Jean Wiseman predicted that Chanel was simply ahead of the trend, asking 'has Chanel lost touch with the time – or is she the one step

Fig. 34 Gabrielle Chanel on the
mirrored staircase of her couture
house, Paris, 1 March 1954.
Photograph by Suzy Parker

Fig. 35 A jersey dress from
Chanel's Spring/Summer 1954
return collection, American *Vogue*,
March 1954. Photograph by
Henry Clarke

ahead…likely to influence much that we shall wear in a year or so?', and
added a warning to Christian Dior that 'Chanel may be one step ahead of
you'.[97] The American fashion press was also, in general, more sympathetic,
recognizing the consistency and easy wearability of Chanel's offering.[98]

In many ways, the collection carried on from where Chanel had left off at
the end of the 1930s: she presented dresses and suits with a relaxed fit in
her favourite jerseys, and in defiance of the prevailing trends (fig.35). Arguably,
however, Chanel also acknowledged the current fashions, with feminine
evening dresses featuring fitted bodices and full skirts (no.46), although even in
these pieces the models appeared to have natural, uncinched waists.

Undeterred by the mixed response, Chanel and Wertheimer agreed that
she should carry on rebuilding the couture business. In May 1954 the pair

Fig. 36 A lace evening dress from Chanel's Autumn/Winter 1954 collection modelled at the Chanel salons in Paris

renegotiated for a final time. Chanel sold him her stakes in both the perfume and couture businesses, along with the Chanel name. In return, all her costs and expenses would be covered, and she would continue to receive the agreed percentage of royalties on worldwide sales.

Perhaps in response to the partial indifference of the press to her Spring collection, for the following season Chanel avoided any mention of a formal showing, instead offering a 'private collection for clients only'.[99] At this exclusive presentation in September 1954 the immediate response was – possibly in part due to a carefully selected invitation list – far more positive. One reporter praised the 'soft, flattering and figure fitting' styles, which 'drew applause from a surprised audience', adding the stinging praise that 'it hardly looked like Chanel at all'.[100] Certainly, this Autumn/Winter collection featured silhouettes attuned to contemporary trends (no.47), but many looks continued to demonstrate a reprise and reimagining of her historic designs, executed sympathetically to the style and silhouettes of the current day. A mid-sleeved, calf-length evening dress of cream lace (fig.36) recalled her simple, youthful designs of the 1930s (for example, no.41), rendered with a contemporary flair.

Following the more favourable reception of her Autumn/Winter 1954 collection, Chanel's position in the western fashion world continued to regain relevance, with approving reviews and an expanding list of new international clients. There was one garment in particular that cemented her widespread success in this period: the suit.

THE SUIT

From her first return collection of Spring 1954, Chanel included her long-standing staple of simple daytime suits. Designed to be neat, comfortable and easy to wear, Chanel's suits had been a part of her oeuvre since the 1920s (see pp.28–30). Once again, she applied her trusted jerseys and tweeds to uncluttered jackets and skirts, teamed with a collared blouse (fig.37). It was these daywear staples, rather than the delicate feminine eveningwear, that piqued the interest of American buyers. Over the next two years, while the overall design of her suits remained consistent, Chanel honed the details and by around 1957 the Chanel suit with all its soon-to-be classic hallmarks emerged, fully formed and instantly recognizable (fig.38).

Chanel's formula for her quintessential suit comprised a straight-cut jacket with a straight just-over-the-knee skirt and a corresponding blouse, which was usually sleeveless. As with most of her garments, Chanel's suits were designed to work with the body and its natural postures. Unlike many couturiers who began designing with sketches that were then translated into dress patterns, Chanel designed directly on the body. This approach enabled her to craft with the body's natural movements in mind. Underlining this imperative to British *Vogue*'s Rosamond Bernier in 1954, Chanel declared 'elegance in clothes means being able to move freely, to do anything with ease'.[101] She sought to create clothes that allowed for an uncompromising freedom of movement, which would not hinder or restrict the wearer as did so many of the corseted and girdled fashions of the day.

A stark point of difference from the stiff and highly sculpted suits of the period was Chanel's rejection of the traditional tailoring techniques of interfacing or canvasing and padding. Instead, she adopted a 'cardigan' cut and, to provide just enough flexible structure, joined the lining to the top fabric with regular vertical lines of stitching. A gilt chain was stitched on the inside hem of her jackets, weighting it just enough so that the jackets always hung elegantly from the shoulders. The positioning of the armhole was also crucial – a high armhole allowed for the freer movement of the arms – and Chanel was apparently keenly preoccupied with getting the placement of the set-in sleeves just right.[102] The approach proved eminently more comfortable and enabled easy, natural movement without disturbing the line of the jacket. Skirt zips were often placed at the back or the side, sometimes in pairs, to ensure the skirt sat perfectly over the waist and hips. Highlighting Chanel's technique in 1957, *Tatler* described the result as a 'very casual woollen suit…straight, unfitted and loose'.[103]

While she employed a range of different collar styles, Chanel's classic choice was a round collarless neckline, which she took care to cut not too high, so as to ensure comfort as well as to elongate the wearer's neck. Pockets, often highlighted with trims matching those of the opening, collar and cuffs of the jacket, added a point of interest and enabled the wearer to adopt the

Fig. 37 A suit from Chanel's Spring/Summer 1954 return collection, *Life* magazine, 1 March 1954. Photograph by Paul Himmel

quintessential Chanel gait, jutting the hips forward with hands nonchalantly placed in one's pockets. Along with the trims, buttons were frequently an important part of the design, but never only decorative: 'no button without a buttonhole'.[104] The jacket and skirt were accompanied by a blouse, usually of a fabric matching the jacket lining, continuing Chanel's designs of the 1920s. Although the blouse was typically sleeveless, Chanel sometimes added a faux shirt cuff attached to the cuff of the jacket sleeve (no.53) or, alternatively, turned back the cuffs of the jacket to show the matching lining (nos 48, 61).

Chanel created a suit for every season and every occasion, using a wide range of fabrics: silks (see no.54), linens and, most commonly, wool tweed. Sourcing textiles from specialist suppliers across Europe, Chanel re-established her pre-war connections with British mills, including Linton Tweeds (see pp.30–1), as well as seeking out modern designs from London-based Ascher Ltd (no.56), and innovative newcomers such as Scotland-based Bernat Klein or self-taught Parisian handweaver Malhia Kent.[105] She continued to prefer supple fabrics with a soft handle that delivered the necessary comfort and ease of movement.

The influence of the Chanel suit was well established by the end of the 1950s, and while not everyone could afford the genuine article, many women across Europe and North America were at least wearing a version of one. In 1958 French *Elle* magazine ran a series revealing the secrets behind the Chanel suit, and the following year provided a dress pattern for their readers to make their own.[106] In Britain the *Daily Mirror* described how Chanel 'cardigan' suits had 'swept the world',[107] and London reporter Jill Bateman wrote:

Fig. 38 House model Paule de
Mérindol poses outside the
Chanel boutique, Paris, 1959

This Spring will go down in fashion history as the year when every woman who considered herself fashionable owned a 'Chanel' suit. Not one bought at great expense from Chanel herself but one of the hundreds of Chanel-inspired designs which are filling the London shops.[108]

The British high-street retailer Wallis produced particularly successful copies of Chanel suits. In the USA Chanel had deals with several department stores and manufacturers including Davidow, which made licensed versions of Chanel designs. There were also floods of unofficial copies using the term 'Chanel suit' as a style descriptor rather than any brand claim. Chanel herself was famously unconcerned with being copied, telling Paul Morand that to be upset by copies would be 'admitting you have run out of ideas'.[109]

By the start of the 1960s, Chanel had once again established herself as a fashion leader. American *Vogue* declared the Chanel suit to be 'the world's prettiest uniform'.[110] As the decade progressed, Chanel adjusted her suits to the emerging trends without compromising the fundamentals of her formula. She expanded the style into eveningwear, creating cocktail suits

Fig. 39 Gabrielle Chanel at work, Paris, 1962. Photograph by Douglas Kirkland

following the same form but made from a plethora of richly decorative fabrics, including gold and silver lamés, textured cloqués and intricately patterned silks (see nos 61, 62 and 67).

THE TOTAL LOOK

Chanel began her career in accessories and, as her style evolved, they remained central to the Chanel look, which was, of course, not complete without jewellery. In the run up to her return collection, in 1953 she approached the jewellery-maker Maison Degorce, which in turn appointed the up-and-coming goldsmith Robert Goossens (1927–2016) to oversee the co-design and creation of pieces for Chanel.[111] Degorce was Chanel's supplier until its closure in 1957, at which point Goossens continued to produce jewellery for Chanel in his own atelier. Her new jewellery designs followed a similar style to her output during the first part of her career, centring around generous strings of imitation pearls, bold brooches awash with colourful glass gems and pendants of rock crystals, each combined with a characteristically abundant approach (see no.58). Chanel also reprised some of her earlier designs with Gripoix from the 1920s and '30s.

Alongside her celebrated costume jewellery, she designed scarves, gloves and handbags. When Chanel relaunched her House in 1954, in order to further simplify her formula for dressing, she decided to create a bag that would be adaptable to all eventualities. With external quilting inspired by equestrian equipment, the bag was offered in lambskin, suede or jersey. Wishing to dispense with the bother of holding a bag in her hand, Chanel ensured that the bag incorporated a strengthened chain shoulder strap, which also gave the decorative effect of jewellery (no.49). Launched in February 1955, in keeping with her fondness for numeric titles she named it the 2.55 handbag.

In 1957 Chanel approached a number of different shoemakers in a quest to design the ultimate Chanel shoe. She finally settled on Massaro, a shoemaker based on rue de la Paix, in order to develop the prototype. Established in 1894, the Massaro House was a discreet address, known by word of mouth and personal recommendation. Raymond Massaro, grandson of the founder, recalled Chanel's relationship with his own father as 'a love story' on professional terms.[112] Chanel strove to simplify, and to discourage the habit of many of her haute couture customers of ordering individual pairs of shoes for each outfit from their own shoemakers. As always, she designed to suit her own wardrobe. She chose a beige leather to match her skin tone, giving the appearance of an elongated leg. A small black toecap gave a tiny punctuation over the toes that visually shortened the foot and protected the paler leather from the dirt of the street (no.51).

Fig. 42 Romy Schneider wears a
Chanel suit and hat in *Boccaccio '70*,
with a bottle of Chanel N°5 in the
foreground, 1963

Fig. 43 Stanley Marcus and
Gabrielle Chanel at the 20th
Annual Neiman Marcus Fashion
Exposition in Dallas, Texas,
9 September 1957

ENDURING INFLUENCE

Chanel's impact on fashion extended to cinema costume once again. Actors
across Europe and North America wore her creations on- and off-screen.
Chanel's creations were chosen for the female leads in countless films in
Europe and the USA, for example Jeanne Moreau in *The Lovers* (1958, directed
by Louis Malle), Delphine Seyrig in *Last Year at Marienbad* (1961, directed by
Alain Resnais; see no.63) and Romy Schneider in director Luchino Visconti's
contribution to the film anthology *Boccaccio '70* (1962; fig.42).

In 1957 the influential American department store Neiman Marcus
cemented the success of Chanel's return by honouring her with an
award for Distinguished Service in the Field of Fashion at its annual
awards ceremony known as the 'Oscars of the fashion industry' (fig.43).[113]
Ultimately, the legacy of Chanel's return to fashion was threefold: her
suit became a timeless staple of western women's wardrobes for years to
come, her two-tone pumps an endlessly adapted style and her handbag a
coveted icon. Her name once again drew respect and authority in Paris,
and the enthusiasm for her designs in the North American market ensured

international success. Following a career spanning more than 60 years, on
10 January 1971 Chanel died at her suite in the Ritz, aged 87.

Chanel's final collection was presented on 26 January 1971, two
weeks after her death (fig.44). Unusually for someone who was noted
for obsessively working on her collections right up until the night before
their presentation, Chanel had already completed 76 models by the time
she died.[114] According to *The Times*:

> It was a beautiful collection, in the best sense of the word. It was Chanel at
> her best. All the hallmarks were there. The pearl earrings, the little hats, the
> pale tweeds flecked with grey, the white pleated crêpes, the gold chains, the
> gardenias, the gilt buttons, the silk shirts, the men's ties.[115]

The collection was widely praised, particularly for the new skirt length,
which sat just below the knee. Despite the loss and upheaval, 'outwardly it
was the same show as ever: the mannequins emerging to wave their numbers
like the sword Excalibur and to set off around the mirror multiplied salon in
the Chanel glide'.[116] The inclusion of light, easy-to-wear evening dresses was
the ultimate finishing touch (see no.73). Fashion writer Alison Adburgham
declared that 'the look of Chanel, casual but elegant, could be the answer
to the modern woman's dilemma',[117] a fitting tribute to a woman who had
spent the last 60 years designing garments to be exactly that.

This soft unstructured hat is made from an open-looped braid stitched into shape; it is collapsible and portable. The lone decoration is a thick silk band with the underside of the brim faced with similar-coloured silk satin. Inside the top of the crown, a drawstring silk lining reveals a large black label woven with yellow text: Gabrielle Chanel, 21 rue Cambon, Paris. The square crown label, usually in black or white silk with a coloured script, was a type used by exclusive millinery establishments, with smaller labels occasionally affixed to the centre back of the internal hat band. The silhouette of this hat with its relaxed loose crown and its narrow brim is close in style to the Chanel hat worn by the actress Gabrielle Dorziat in the March 1913 issue of *Les Modes* magazine. Dorziat was a friend of Chanel's from her Royallieu days and an important patron of her work. With her wardrobe drawing much scrutiny, Dorziat's wearing of Chanel hats both on stage and off attracted the attention of fashionable clients and the press. **OC**

1. HAT

SPRING/SUMMER 1917
SILK
PATRIMOINE DE CHANEL,
PARIS: ACC.HC.PE.1917.1

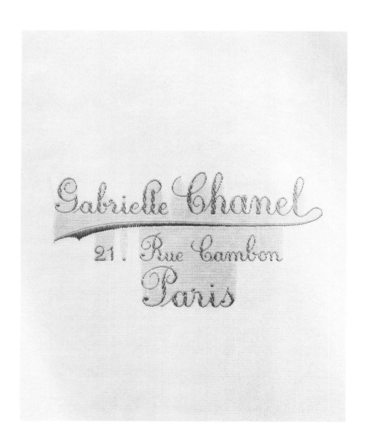

Previous spread

Fig. 45 Chanel labels, 1910–69.
Patrimoine de CHANEL, Paris

Fig. 46 Silk hat label, *c.*1910.
Patrimoine de CHANEL, Paris:
DOC.MOD.4577

Jersey made Chanel's name a force to be reckoned with in the world of French fashion. She was the first to openly celebrate the humble fabric, utilizing wool jersey in its neutral undyed colour probably sourced from textile manufacturer Rodier. The ever-innovative Chanel soon adopted silk jersey as a lighter more fluid option for her summer garments, with *Vogue* noting 'Chanel who is already famous for her staunch fidelity to jersey, is making a stir just now by her individual use of jersey-de-soie [silk jersey]'.[1] One of the earliest extant Chanel garments, this blouse of 1916, also referred to in the fashion press of the time as a jacket, is made from fine-gauge silk jersey. Previously used as a textile for underwear and stockings, Chanel was the first to demonstrate the appeal and ease of silk jersey for entire garments. With its softly draped structure and non-constricting silk tie belt, the blouse is constructed in a flat T-shape, its only decoration being a sailor collar and turned-back cuffs. This garment would have been worn as part of a suit with a gathered skirt. In summer 1916 *Vogue* published illustrations of two Chanel silk jersey suits, one in greige and another in cream, and a third in 'old blue jersey' with a jacket of the same simple construction, belted but without buttons or fastenings, made to be 'drawn on over the head'.[2] **OC**

2. BLOUSE

SPRING/SUMMER 1916
SILK JERSEY
PATRIMOINE DE CHANEL,
PARIS: HC.PE.1916.1

Fig. 47 Gabrielle Chanel standing in front of her boutique, Deauville, 1913

Planche III. — TAILLEURS DE JEUNES FILLES. — *Modèles des "Élégances Parisiennes" (fig. 81, 82 et 83)*

garni de galon ciré noir. Doublure de satin ciré apparaissant au col.

Fig. 84. Robe de faille bleu foncé lamée d'or. Dentelle d'or au corsage. Traîne de tulle noir, alourdie de dentelle d'or (Lelong).

Fig. 85. Robe de mousseline de soie blanche bordée d'une large dentelle d'argent posée sur un ruban bleu, tunique de Chantilly noir, corsage de dentelle d'argent, ceinture de ruban bleu-nattier (Berthe et Hermance. Dentelle de Thiébault).

Fig. 86. Déshabillé de taffetas glacé rose ; ceinture et col en faille

d'un ton plus soutenu (Chéruit).

Fig. 87. Robe de tulle, bordée de filet ourlé d'un volant d'organdi ; ceinture en ruban de faille, de deux tons de bleu. Ruban N° 255 de la Maison Blum. Dentelle Myra de la Maison Marescot.

Fig. 88. Robe de taffetas tricolore sur un dessous de Chantilly blanc (Marescot), ruban de velours noir. Tissu N° 19116 A (Bianchini et Férier).

Fig. 89. Robe de Malines ; ceinture lamée blanc, or et argent ; ruban broché. Dentelle Radium de la Maison Marescot ; ruban 2549 de la Maison

Blum ; tissu de la Maison Bianchini et Férier.

Fig. 90. Chapeau de faille grège, plumes assorties (Lewis).

Fig. 91. Chapeau de paille anglaise noire, calotte de satin bleu vif. Motif noir et bleu (Lewis).

Fig. 92. Chapeau de satin gris-argent orné sur le devant de deux galons d'argent (Lewis).

Fig. 93. Grand canotier de taffetas glacé amaranthe, garni de franges de soie du même ton. Gros pavot de taffetas sur le devant (Lewis).

Fig. 94. Grand chapeau de taffetas vieux rose du Barry, doublé de taffetas taupe. Motif en ruban picot rose et taupe (Lewis).

Fig. 48 Chanel models featured in
Les Élégances Parisiennes, May 1916

3. DRESS

AUTUMN/WINTER 1918
SILK, LAMÉ, JET BEADS, SEQUINS
PATRIMOINE DE CHANEL, PARIS:
HC.AH.1918.2

This sophisticated and timeless evening dress was designed by Chanel in 1918. It bears many of the hallmarks of her eveningwear, such as the square neckline, slim shoulder straps and the shimmering sequinned and beaded surface, that would appear in her designs over the coming decades. In places, a gold lamé under-dress shines through the undulating lines of the embellished surface. A heavy jet-beaded fringe hangs from the end of the tulle waist sash and the edge of the skirt opening, which trails away into a beaded train. Fringes seemed to overwhelm the *Vogue* correspondent who noted that in Paris of 1919, 'Fringes black and fringes white, fringes from the neckline to the hem of the skirt…fringes, fringes, fringes, in short much too many fringes'.[3] Yet this particularly glamorous jet fringe may have escaped censure, as the author went on to concede that few things were 'more becoming than the dark mysterious sparkle of black jet'.[4] **OC**

In September 1919 *Vogue* commented on a new trend for lace: 'For afternoon dresses there is nothing so popular at the present moment as lace, of which there has been a veritable renaissance'.[5] Among the models chosen to illustrate the point was this Chanel afternoon dress of Chantilly lace. Composed of two pieces, a blouse with a scallop-edged pelmet and an under-dress, it shows classic elements of Chanel's design hallmarks in the deep V-neck collar, tiered skirt and play on transparency with unlined lace sleeves. Widely used in haute couture, Chantilly lace is celebrated for its delicate naturalistic floral depictions. Originally a bobbin lace made by hand, from the nineteenth century companies such as Marescot produced fine mechanized versions on Leavers lace machines. For the fashionable racegoers of 1919, this style of afternoon dress was a popular choice, with the press recording 'on the great race days at the end of the season one saw innumerable models in black, white and beige lace, in some form of tiered or flounced skirt'.[6] One such wearer was Lady Victoria Bullock, who was pictured in June in a beige-coloured version at the fashionable Longchamp racecourse.[7] **OC**

4. DRESS

SPRING/SUMMER 1919
CHANTILLY LACE
PATRIMOINE DE CHANEL,
PARIS: HC.PE.1919.3

Fig. 49 Chantilly lace gown by
Chanel, American *Vogue*, 1 September
1919. Illustration by Claire Avery

5. DRESS

SPRING/SUMMER 1919
SILK GEORGETTE, CHIFFON
PATRIMOINE DE CHANEL,
PARIS: HC.INC.1919.1

Fig. 50 Racegoers at Deauville wearing
Chanel, 10 August 1919. Photograph
by Séeberger Frères

In the aftermath of the First World War, fashion for women changed dramatically. In March 1919 *Vogue* commented on Chanel's new modern silhouette that there was 'an alarming tendency for dresses to come down at the top and go up at the bottom. Not since the days of the Bourbons has the woman of fashion been so visible above the ankles.'[8] This light georgette and chiffon summer dress exemplifies this modern trend with its short skirt, low V-neckline and simple T-shaped silhouette. It was the perfect garment to wear at the fashionable seaside resort of Deauville, as captured in a fashion reportage photograph by the Séeberger brothers in August 1919, worn loosely belted with a chiffon sash. The simplicity of this line contrasts vividly with the intricate decoration of the skirt. Here, complex cutwork roses, comprised of picot-edged, silk georgette petals, are embroidered with miniature pearls and suspended to create voided floral motifs all over the skirt. Along the neckline tiny hand-stitched pearl beading adds subtle detailing. These pearl decorations are also sewn onto the transparent chiffon trim on the edge of the sleeves. **OC**

6. DRESS

1920-1
SILK, SEQUINS, BEADS
PATRIMOINE DE CHANEL,
PARIS: HC.INC.1920-1921.1

Chanel's eveningwear for 1920 and 1921 was noted for its elegant lines. The silhouette of this dress closely follows the body apart from a small pleated section of georgette and tulle emerging at either side of the skirt, as though peeking out from behind an apron. Press descriptions of the Paris collections in May 1921 highlighted that, 'the apron effects which have appeared in several collections are used on some Chanel models, and it is to be noted that they form part of the gown itself'.[9] The inference of an apron in this dress is clear, albeit one that is lavishly decorated with beading and sequins. The curved hem of the vertically sequinned skirt panel hangs over a plain georgette skirt with gold thread embroidery around the hem. These richly embellished curved panels on both the bodice and the skirt give an opulence and sophistication to the minimal evening silhouette. **OC**

The visual identity of Chanel N°5 was just as innovative as the scent inside (see pp.22–4). In contrast to the highly decorative, Nouveau-inspired fantasy creations of other perfumiers of the time, Chanel chose the simplest, cleanest form for her perfume bottle. Reminiscent of medicine vials, the original Chanel N°5 bottle from 1921 is an unadorned rectangular glass container. The only decoration is on the stopper: two interlocking Cs enclosed in a circle – the first time Chanel used what would become an iconic symbol. A plain square label gives only the essential information. When the production of Chanel N°5 expanded in 1924, Chanel refined her bottle design only slightly. The square stopper became octagonal, supposedly inspired by the Place Vendôme, and the sharp shoulders of the bottle became bevelled, and therefore less liable to break. The labelling, packaging and typography of Chanel perfume and beauty products have remained true to Chanel's initial vision, germinated by this bottle. With its stark white and black label, sans serif capitals, linear shape and lack of other adornment, it is remarkable that this strict, simple design looks as invitingly modern today as it did more than one hundred years ago. **CKB**

The streamlined modernism inherent in the design of the Chanel perfume bottle is amplified in the reflective surfaces and sharp lines of these limited edition nickel chrome cases from 1921 to the 1930s. Chanel also offered a matching line of make-up accessories with silver lids and cases. **OC**

7. CHANEL N°5 BOTTLE

1921
GLASS, WAX, COTTON THREAD
PATRIMOINE DE CHANEL,
PARIS: C.1.643

Overleaf
8. PERFUMES AND BEAUTY PRODUCTS

1921–39
GLASS, NICKEL CHROME, POLYMER
PATRIMOINE DE CHANEL, PARIS

The intricate embroidery covering this tunic blouse of Spring/Summer 1922 was probably carried out by the House of Kitmir (see p.21). Kitmir was established by the Russian Grand Duchess Maria Pavlovna Romanova. It was after meeting Chanel and visiting her atelier that Pavlovna decided to use her talent for embroidery, learnt as a hobby during her privileged childhood, to make a living for herself. Previously, the exiled Grand Duchess had made the most of her knitting skills to produce sweaters for a London boutique, prior to relocating to Paris.[10] At her Kitmir atelier she employed other Russian émigrés to embroider elaborate embellishments for the couture houses of Paris, drawing on techniques and motifs common to the stitched decoration of central and eastern European traditional dress. Chanel worked with Kitmir on several collections, including embroideries for her 1922 Spring/Summer collection, where she applied the embroideries to blouses, tunics and coats in shapes with similar inspiration. This blouse, teamed with a plain black skirt, was illustrated in *Vogue* alongside the following description: 'Chanel turns to the Balkans not only for embroideries, but for the lines of the blouse itself'.[11] Grand Duchess Pavlovna was awarded a Gold Medal and an honorary diploma for her embroidery work at the Exhibition of Contemporary Decorative and Industrial Arts in 1925. At the end of the decade, she sold Kitmir to the embroidery house Fritel et Hurel and left Paris. **CKB**

9. BLOUSE

SPRING/SUMMER 1922
CREPE DE CHINE
PATRIMOINE DE CHANEL,
PARIS: HC.PE.1922.4

Fig. 51 Chanel outfit with embroidery by Kitmir, French *Vogue*, April 1922. Illustration by Reynaldo Luza

Elaborate machine embroidery covers this wool twill coat, providing a uniform pattern of vertical decoration. Adding visual interest, Chanel employed the pattern horizontally on the sleeves, shoulders and hem of the coat. Its use on the reverse of the turned-back cuffs maintained a consistent finish. The abstract but regimented motifs in this design are typical of the embroideries produced by the House of Kitmir for Chanel at this time (see p.21). The colours of the coat are complemented by the beige and brown of its fur collar. Another Chanel coat with a similar all-over embroidery, but shorter and simpler in design, was illustrated in *Vogue* in spring 1922. **CKB**

10. COAT

*c.*1922–3
WOOL, SILK, FUR
PATRIMOINE DE CHANEL,
PARIS: HC.INC.1922–1923.2

Fig. 52 An embroidered coat by Chanel, American *Vogue*, March 1922. Illustration by Harriet Meserole

11. DRESS

SPRING/SUMMER 1923
EMBROIDERED SILK GEORGETTE,
GLASS BEADS, GILT THREAD
V&A: T.86-1974
GIVEN BY THE HON. MRS ANTHONY
HENLEY

Dating from Chanel's Spring/Summer collection of 1923, this dress is covered in a striking embroidery design probably carried out by the House of Kitmir (see p.21; nos 9 and 10). Couched gilt frisé thread is combined with clear bugle beads in a graphic design comprising a central circular motif on the bodice (echoed on the back) and repeating stripes of decoration on the skirt. These stripes are extended onto tabs of chiffon projecting from either side of the skirt, punctuating the otherwise straight and simple silhouette. A square-shaped bodice with a low waist, typical of this period, is defined solely by the placement of the embroidery pattern. The silk georgette gives a light and delicate feel to the dress despite the extensive decoration. The skirt of the dress is open from the knee down, making it easy to move freely: a staple feature of Chanel's approach to designing clothes. An integral black silk petticoat is edged with a thin band of intricate black lace. A sketch of a similar design is in the collection of Henri Bendel, a New York department store that was one of the first retailers of Chanel designs in the USA. **CKB**

Fig. 53 Sketch of a Chanel dress, Spring/
Summer 1923. Henri Bendel Collection,
Brooklyn Museum, New York

12/13. BATHING COSTUMES

1924
WOOL
V&A: S.836–1980, S.837–1980
GIVEN BY THE FRIENDS OF THE MUSEUM
OF PERFORMANCE

In 1924 Chanel designed the costumes, including these two bathing suits, for Serge Diaghilev's ballet *Le Train Bleu*. The hand-knitted pink suit with black-and-white bands of different widths on the skirt and legs was created for the character of La Perlouse danced by Lydia Sokolova. The blue jersey suit was one of a group designed for the Gigolos of the corps de ballet. Although they appear to be separates, both suits are one-piece designs, each with a simple hook-and-eye opening on the left shoulder. Chanel paired the pink suit with a neat suede skullcap and large, heavy pearl-effect earrings. Driven by fashion rather than practical dance considerations, Sokolova recalled in her autobiography how the earrings were painful to wear and the rubber bathing shoes – which replaced ballet shoes in the name of authenticity – difficult to dance in.[12] The ballet involved Sokolova being thrown into the air and being caught by her partner Leon Woizikovski (the Golfer), who found it almost impossible to grip the slippery woollen fabric. Despite these challenges, this costume and the others that Chanel designed for the ballet did exactly as intended, capturing the bathing, golfing and tennis-playing lifestyles of the fashionable Riviera set. **OC**

Fig. 54 *Le Train Bleu*, performed by
Serge Diaghilev's Ballets Russes, June
1924. V&A: S.294–2017, Cyril W.
Beaumont Bequest

Black was a staple for Chanel's eveningwear throughout her career, and she regularly played with black-on-black embellishment, balancing opulence with simplicity. This monochrome dress, from her Spring/Summer 1926 collection, showcases abundant decoration of sequins and jet beading. The entire bottom half of the dress is covered in strips of sparkling black sequins, arranged in tiers punctuated by horizontal strips of diagonally placed jet barrel beads. The final tier ends at the low thigh, where the sequined strips cascade freely over the legs. The bodice includes a bolero edged with sequins and beads, which is attached at the front and hangs away from the body at the back. The dress was featured extensively in the press. French *Vogue* described it as a 'marvellous dress' that was 'especially interesting for the movement of its bolero and the effect of its long skirt'.[13] The magazine included an illustration of the Marquise de Jaucourt wearing the dress. The Marquise was a member of the fashionable set who frequently appeared in French society pages and was a friend of Count Étienne de Beaumont (see p.35). American *Vogue* included a photograph by Edward Steichen of model Marion Morehouse wearing the dress, and noted the asymmetrical hemline achieved through longer sequined fringes on the left side. **CKB**

14. DRESS

SPRING/SUMMER 1926
SILK CREPE GEORGETTE, JET, SEQUINS
PATRIMOINE DE CHANEL, PARIS:
HC.PE.1926.4

Fig. 55 Illustration of the Marquise de Jaucourt wearing a dress by Chanel, French *Vogue*, June 1926

16

Cette merveilleuse robe de Chanel, portée par la Marquise de Jaucourt, est intéressante surtout par son mouvement de boléro et l'effet de jupe longue, presque une jupe orientale, dû à des franges de crêpe Georgette brodées de jais

Fig. 56 Marion Morehouse, American
Vogue, 1 May 1926. Photograph by
Edward Steichen

In 1926 actress Ina Claire was photographed by
Edward Steichen for *Vogue* in a version of this 'glittering
gown'. This particular dress, which belonged to Grace,
Marchioness Curzon of Kedleston, is entirely embellished
with sequinned floral motifs that graduate in size from
the shoulder to the hem. Embroidered in two parts with
a break at the waist, a streamer of black chiffon flares
out from the hip. This swathe of lightweight fabric was
a typical Chanel feature at the time, adding drama and
movement to her narrow evening silhouettes. At the
front of the dress, the low V-neckline is infilled with a
black chiffon modesty piece. At the back, the neckline
is cut low beneath the shoulder blades. Such exuberant
surface embellishment was unusual for Chanel. Although
she used all-over sequin embroidery, she tended to focus
predominantly on monochrome surfaces. *The Times* noted
in 1929 that Chanel's eveningwear took the form of
'dresses in coloured sequins, so closely set as to look like
fish scales'.[14] **OC**

15. DRESS
SPRING/SUMMER 1926
SILK, CHIFFON, TULLE, SEQUINS
DERBY MUSEUMS: 1974–960/24
GIFT OF THE CURZON FAMILY

16. DRESS

c.1926
SILK CHIFFON
DERBY MUSEUMS: 1974–960.17
GIFT OF THE CURZON FAMILY

This classic black Chanel evening dress belonged to Grace, Marchioness Curzon of Kedleston, who purchased a number of dresses from Chanel in 1926. Her selection of garments included several black and some white dresses in the lightest of chiffons and silks, along with other more elaborate dresses, such as an entirely sequinned dress (see no.15) and one decorated with long fringed tassels. A wealthy heiress with a great interest in fashion, the Marchioness had lost her second husband in 1925 and her daughter was to be launched as a debutante in 1926.[15] In light of the mourning period, it is possible that she sought out Chanel for her celebrated expertise in monochrome dressing (both black and white were acceptable mourning colours). This black evening dress is cleverly constructed with asymmetric flared panels falling from the right shoulder and the left hip; these panels are trapped into the body of the dress with careful diagonal lines of seaming creating a graphic lined pattern across the dress. Attached at each shoulder, a loop streamer falls down over the back. A flourish of embellishment is provided by a black chiffon flower pinned to the shoulder, an important source of decoration for Chanel, providing a punctuation to the modernity of her designs. **OC**

Fig. 58 A Chanel dress, French *Vogue*, 1 October 1925. Illustration by Mainbocher

The mid-1920s saw Chanel using silk fringing extensively in her eveningwear. Arranged in tiers across the body and in generous lengths, the fringing emphasized the wearer's every move. For the autumn of 1926, *The Bystander* declared fringing to be '*the* trimming of the moment'.[16] That same season *The Graphic* reported that 'Chanel now thinks in fringes'.[17] This dress was featured in American *Vogue*, which drew attention to 'the graceful way in which the deep shaded fringe is treated'.[18] Indeed, one journalist reporting on the dress for the American press asked, 'Who but Chanel would have evolved shaded fringes? And how strikingly beautiful they are!'[19] The dress comprises two tiers of silk fringing that has been dyed in a gradation from pale blue to dark blue and sewn onto a ground of mid-blue silk georgette crepe. The tiers dip at the centre front and back, creating an even, curved hemline. The top tier forms a shawl back that could be arranged to the wearer's preference: either left to hang from each shoulder or draped asymmetrically over one. Chanel wore a version of this dress at the Duke of Westminster's country house, Eaton Hall. It must have been something of a favourite as, reportedly, Chanel had three versions in different colours.[20] Later in the decade, vivid blue became so associated with Chanel that fashion magazines began referring to it simply as 'Chanel blue'.[21]

CKB

17. DRESS

AUTUMN/WINTER 1926
SILK GEORGETTE CREPE, SILK FRINGING
PATRIMOINE DE CHANEL,
PARIS: HC.AH.1926.4

Fig. 59 Chanel fringed dress, *Harper's Bazaar*, October 1926. Illustration by Reynaldo Luza

Chanel's costume jewellery was an integral part of her fashion offering from the early 1920s onwards (see p.35). This necklace and earrings set comprising geometric gems of glass is of a style that became popular for Chanel in the late 1920s. The minimal settings show off the imitation diamond rhinestones to great effect, enhancing the fashionable Art Deco feel. In 1927 the newspaper *Paris-Midi* commented that 'the latest fashionable necklace launched by Chanel consists of large rhinestone gems', adding that 'in the light, nothing has more sparkle'.[22] The following year, the British magazine *Britannia and Eve* advised, 'last year's Chanel round-beaded crystal necklace should be put away and pearls worn instead, or one of the new Chanel necklaces of triangular pieces of crystal'.[23]

CKB

18. NECKLACE AND EARRINGS

SPRING/SUMMER 1928
SILVER, GLASS
PATRIMOINE DE CHANEL,
PARIS: ACC.HC.PE.1928.2

19. DRESS AND JACKET SUIT

SPRING/SUMMER 1926–7
SILK TAFFETA
PATRIMOINE DE CHANEL,
PARIS: HC.PE.1926–1927.1

Fig. 60 Pencil and watercolour sketch
of a Chanel suit with fabric swatch,
c.1926. Patrimoine de CHANEL, Paris

A simple summer outfit in cream silk, this dress and jacket ensemble is typical of Chanel's mid-1920s daywear, featuring a low, belted waist, pleated skirt and open jacket. Contrasting with the monochrome jacket and skirt and creating Chanel's classic colour combination is a generous bow of black silk taffeta pinned to the left shoulder. Crenelated edges, executed with astonishing precision, feature on the turned-back cuffs and collar of the jacket and hem of the bodice. This notched decoration epitomizes a distinctly Chanel approach. Rather than embellishing with an addition such as a ribbon trim, embroidery, print or colour, Chanel devised a subtle but nonetheless beautiful detail that was achieved with no added element other than the great technical skill of the seamstresses in her atelier. The exactitude of the crenelations on the hem of the bodice is matched by the sharp narrow box pleats of the skirt. Describing summer outfits in June 1926, *Vogue* recommended skirts with 'the simple inverted pleat beloved by Chanel' that would promise both elegance and ease of movement.[24] This outfit was offered in a range of colours including green.

CKB

20. SUIT

1927–9
WOOL TWEED
PATRIMOINE DE CHANEL, PARIS:
HC.INC.1927–1929.1

Fig. 61 Tweed suit by Chanel (right),
French *Vogue*, 1 April 1927. Illustration
by Lee Creelman Erickson

In November 1926 a double-page spread devoted to six Chanel tweed models featured in *Vogue* with a headline stating that, 'Tweed is an essential of the smart new wardrobe',[25] emphasizing its suitability for both town- and country-wear. This skirt suit from *c.*1927 exemplifies Chanel's use of tweed in this period. The fabric is surprisingly lightweight and pliable in contrast to the heavier weight of traditional tweed garments. On first glance it seems to be a regular tweed pattern known as a barleycorn weave in white and beige, but due to floating warp threads, from a distance a very subtle windowpane check appears. There is an asymmetry to the suit, with the jacket opening set slightly to the left-hand side. The jacket has a horizontal waist seam just above the flapped patch pockets, which recall those on the traditional Norfolk jacket worn for hunting. Chanel's quest for the best fabric saw her sourcing tweed from many different manufacturers over the years. However, she had a particularly long-lasting relationship with Linton Tweeds of Cumbria, which began in the mid-1920s and continued throughout the rest of her career. **OC**

From the mid-1920s, advertisements and editorials recommending Chanel handbags appeared regularly in the fashion press. Many of these bags took the form of a structured frame with a top handle similar to this example from 1928. Tiny gold loops on the frame indicate where the now missing handle would have been attached. A sample of fabric from the V&A collection shows the original colourway of the handbag, which has faded through time and use. During this period Chanel produced handbags in a variety of materials, from the softest suede to Chanel's own print fabrics, often with matching accessories such as scarves and belts. In 1928 the *Tatler* magazine noted 'the chief characteristic of Chanel's bags is novelty', highlighting several Chanel handbags available from the Fortnum & Mason department store, including two made from a printed Chanel textile design of overlapping square sheets, similar to this bag, with a matching scarf in the same print. **OC**

21. BAG

1928–9
PRINTED WOOL AND SILK, METAL
PATRIMOINE DE CHANEL, PARIS:
ACC.HC.INC.1928–1929.1

Fig. 62 Textile sample of printed wool and silk, Tissus Chanel, Asnières, 1928. V&A: T.191–1975, given by Manchester Design Registry

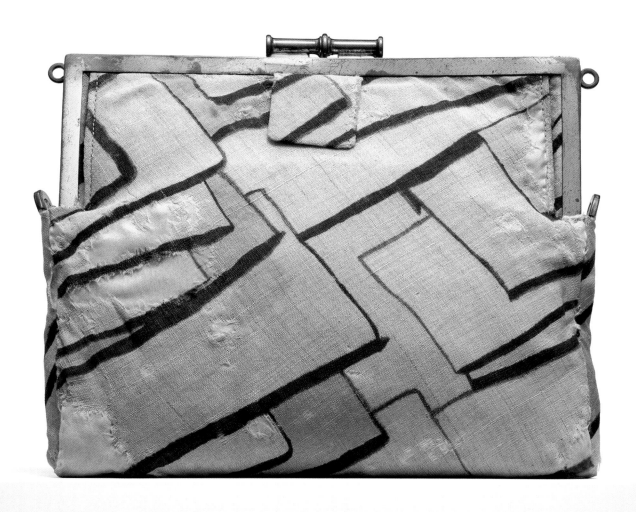

Minoru, Lady Foley, was a young, wealthy widow who indulged her love of Parisian couture, with Chanel and Vionnet among her favoured houses. 'Well known as a hostess and one of the best dressed women in London Society in the 1920s and 1930s',[26] ballroom dancing was a favourite pastime and many of the dresses she ordered have floaty skirts and flounces that moved to great effect on the dance floor. Lady Foley owned this dress in two colourways, a light peach and a deep blue. It is remarkable for the high-shine paillettes that cover the bodice and hips and gradually fade into the flared tulle skirt giving a wet-look sheen. Like many Chanel evening garments of the time, the dress was designed to be worn with a matching transparent tulle shawl. As *The New York Times* noted of Chanel, 'she is a past mistress at the taming of tulle – be it tailored or fluffy'.[27] **OC**

22. DRESS
AUTUMN/WINTER 1929
SILK TULLE, SEQUINS
PATRIMOINE DE CHANEL, PARIS:
HC.AH.1929.5

Fig. 63 Lady Minoru Foley wearing a dress by Chanel, *c.*1932

23. DRESS AND SCARF ENSEMBLE

*c.*1930
PRINTED CREPE DE CHINE
PALAIS GALLIERA, PARIS: 1968.40.91
GIFT OF THE HEIRS OF THE DUCHESSE
DE TALLEYRAND-PÉRIGORD, NÉE ANNA GOULD

For summer dresses Chanel opted for supple textiles such as muslin, pongee, cotton cheesecloth or crepe de Chine, which were commonly used for lounge pyjamas, negligees and even underwear. The very light drape, combined with cuts favouring asymmetrical skirts and subtle ruffles, created fluid silhouettes. Matching stoles or scarves placed freely around the shoulders or neck added movement to the garments, giving a feeling of spontaneity. Here, the minimalist two-tone graphic floral print recalls Chanel's predilection for refining motifs to their essentials. This taste for radicalism in textile decoration is evident in the designs created for Tissus Chanel throughout the 1930s, reaching a peak in 1933 (see p.31). **VB**

24. DRESS

SPRING/SUMMER 1930
COTTON BRODERIE ANGLAISE, SILK
MUSLIN, SILK TULLE
PALAIS GALLIERA, PARIS: 1968.40.113A
GIFT OF THE HEIRS OF THE DUCHESSE DE
TALLEYRAND-PÉRIGORD, NÉE ANNA GOULD

This broderie anglaise dress was photographed by Man Ray in 1930, along with another design by Chanel of muslin and lace. In the image the models wear the two immaculate dresses styled with bonnets adorned with a white feather, as well as long, pale evening gloves and pearl necklaces. Man Ray surrounded the models with opaline white balloons. Everything about the image contributes to a feeling of lightness, naturalness and youth, qualities synonymous with Chanel's designs. Broderie anglaise was considered a modern alternative to more traditional types of lace at the time. Less fragile than conventional lace and usually white, broderie anglaise is often used to make children's clothes. Here, it adds a sense of innocence to the evening dress, the hem and neckline of which are cut to follow the floral motifs of the fabric. Fine gathers at the centre front and light draping over the hips add a more sophisticated note. **VB**

In April 1926 *Vogue* declared, 'Chanel continues to give prominence to flowers – flowers of muslin, large carnations of fabric, to which this year she adds bouquets of wildflowers, poppies, daisies and cornflowers.'[28] The refined elegance of this dress lies in the delicate application of petals and leaf motifs, carefully cut and scalloped, which have been applied meticulously around the neckline, waist and on the hems of the three tiers of the skirt. This particular technique recurs in Chanel designs from the late 1920s for light summer dresses in printed fabrics, usually of muslin. Between embroidery and inlay, this floral appliqué decoration favours lightness while retaining the essence of the motif. For such day dresses Chanel often produced matching coats, lined with the same print as that of the dress and featuring the same appliqué technique with cut-out floral motifs decorating the collar and opening. Chanel later reprised this technique in her creations of the 1950s and '60s. **VB**

25. DRESS

SPRING/SUMMER 1930
PRINTED SILK CHIFFON
PALAIS GALLIERA, PARIS: 1968.40.108
GIFT OF THE HEIRS OF THE DUCHESSE DE
TALLEYRAND-PÉRIGORD, NÉE ANNA GOULD

Fig. 64 Anne Freshman wearing a
Chanel dress, American *Vogue*, 7 June
1930. Photograph by Edward Steichen

26. DRESS

SPRING/SUMMER 1930
PRINTED SILK CHIFFON, APPLIQUÉ
FLORAL MOTIFS
PALAIS GALLIERA, PARIS: 1968.40.190
GIFT OF THE HEIRS OF THE DUCHESSE DE
TALLEYRAND-PÉRIGORD, NÉE ANNA GOULD

This dress is from the wardrobe of Anna, Duchess of Talleyrand-Périgord (1875–1961), daughter of Jay Gould, an American railroad magnate. Anna and her first husband, Boni de Castellane, commissioned a grand mansion, the Palais Rose, located on avenue Foch in Paris. There they hosted sumptuous receptions attended by many of those moving in international elite circles. The dress was donated to the collection of the Palais Galliera in 1968, shortly before the Palais Rose was demolished. The donation included eight dresses by Chanel dating from between 1928 and 1935 (see nos 23–5 and 27). With an elegance imbued with originality but without eccentricity, the garments reflect Chanel's combination of simplicity and touches of complexity that characterizes her creations of the 1920s and '30s. The straight silhouette of the dress is typical of Chanel's designs in this period. Here, the appliqué floral motifs reveal an attention to detail that was much praised by the press. **VB**

27. DRESS AND BOLERO

SPRING/SUMMER 1930
PRINTED SILK CANVAS
PALAIS GALLIERA, PARIS: 1968.40.92AB
GIFT OF THE HEIRS OF THE DUCHESSE DE
TALLEYRAND-PÉRIGORD, NÉE ANNA GOULD

Polka dots became a classic pattern associated with chic style in the 1930s. In February 1929 *Vogue* noted: 'polka dots appear again on all fabrics, and the crepe satin with tiny dots will certainly be a great success. There is something new even in the most familiar motifs.'[29] Given the simple and abstract nature of polka dots, it is not surprising that they appealed to Chanel's design sensibility. For this dress, she combined the polka dot motif with a bright red, a colour that was a constant presence in her collections. This ensemble comprises a skirt and bodice in silk pongee with a matching bolero in a straight silhouette. Any hint of severity is balanced by the finely pleated ruffles. Arranged around the neckline and at the edges of the bodice and cuffs, the ruffles soften the line and bring a sense of movement. Ensuring lightness, the ruffles are mounted on an inlaid tape, unhemmed but finished in small, delicate points. Soft bows placed at the centre front are one of Chanel's recurring motifs, adorning dresses, suits and even jewellery. **VB**

This silk day dress in Chanel's signature ivory-and-black palette is decorated with a soft blurred dot pattern. Although this gives the effect of a pattern integral to the weave, it is in fact a printed design applied after the fabric had been woven. The dress incorporates numerous details such as bows, pleats, bias-cut piecing and pockets, illustrating that Chanel was moving away from the austerity of her earlier years towards a more subtly romantic phase which would develop in her work of the 1930s. The visible feature pocket, as seen on this dress, was one of the numerous facets of menswear that Chanel incorporated into her daywear. It even became a prop for her own famous stance, one hand jammed into a pocket while the other gesticulated. In 1938 English fashion journalist Jean Burnup commented on Chanel's signature attitude, 'insolently watching her own show from the backstairs, one hand mannishly thrust into a skirt pocket, the other fiddling with a match box, and giving it, in some indescribable way…chic'.[30] **OC**

28. DRESS

c.1930–9
SILK
PATRIMOINE DE CHANEL, PARIS:
HC.INC.1930–1939.14

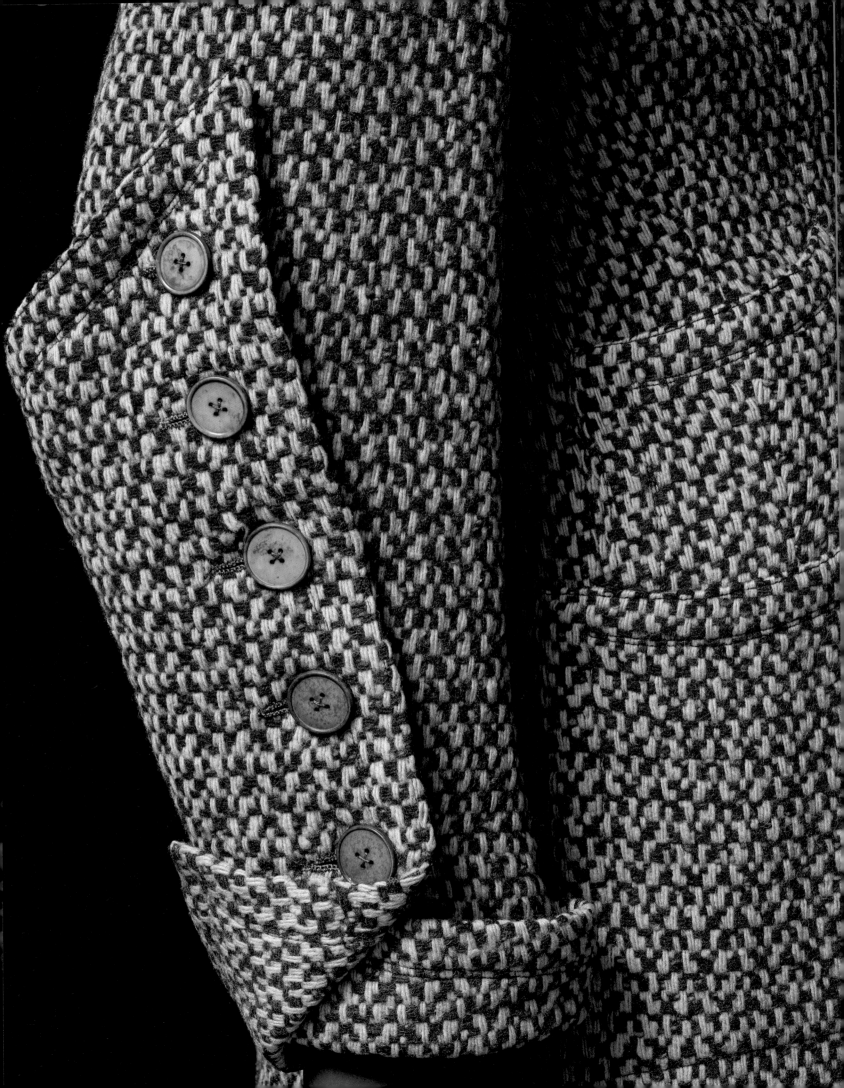

29. COAT

AUTUMN/WINTER 1933
WOOL TWEED
PATRIMOINE DE CHANEL, PARIS:
HC.AH.1933.3

This purple-and-white tweed overcoat has a deep purple silk lining and a matching tweed skirt, which is narrow at the waist and flares out towards the hem. Reporting on winter fashions for 1933, the press noted that Patou, Vionnet and Chanel had all designed coats that had sleeves, shoulders and collars that were 'invariably novel'.[31] This coat follows that example with its asymmetrical shawl collar, button opening that sits to the left and unusually detailed sleeves. Below the elbow the arms appear to have winged tweed gauntlets tapering into turned-back cuffs. These are attached with a vertical row of buttons. These specially dyed buttons, along with those that fasten the front opening, have faded over time from purple to bright green. **OC**

Fig. 65 Sketch of a Chanel coat,
Autumn/Winter 1933. Henri Bendel
Collection, Brooklyn Museum,
New York

30. DRESS

1935
WOOL JERSEY, ALBENE RIB KNIT, METAL
PALAIS GALLIERA, PARIS: 1968.55.37
GIFT OF THE HEIRS OF MR HENRY VIGUIER

Asymmetry was a principle that Chanel favoured in the cut of her designs, particularly during the first part of her career. In contrast to the stability of symmetry, she considered these decentred creations more alive and natural, with a visual tension, added movement and a relaxed look. In this day dress of 1935, the two lines of buttons arranged at an angle to the side give a sense of energy and vitality. The removable white cuffs and collar – which allowed for ease of laundering – are another feature of Chanel's designs, especially for her suits. This dress also highlights Chanel's continued use of jersey. British debutante Lady Pamela Smith wears a similar dress in a photograph taken at Chanel's couture salon in Paris in 1932. Smith stands beside Chanel, who is sitting among a group of young British society women waiting to be fitted ahead of Chanel's London fashion show. **VB**

Fig. 66 Gabrielle Chanel (centre) with
Lady Pamela Smith (standing) and other
society models in the haute couture salons,
31 rue Cambon, Paris, 1932

In the early 1930s, form-fitting satin became a popular evening choice. While Chanel herself favoured white satin as an evening option, she used numerous other shades in her eveningwear designs. Throughout the early twentieth century, the particular pale pink of this ensemble was associated with lingerie and underwear. Chanel frequently used the colour in her evening dresses, with figure-hugging silhouettes and transparent fabrics that blurred the lines between the boudoir and the public arena. The soft flowing skirt and the draping shoulder cape give a relaxed insouciance to the ensemble. **OC**

31. DRESS AND CAPE

*c.*1930–1
SILK SATIN
PATRIMOINE DE CHANEL, PARIS:
HC.INC.1930–1931.4

32. DRESS

SPRING/SUMMER 1930
SILK, LACE, SATIN, TULLE
PATRIMOINE DE CHANEL, PARIS:
HC.PE.1930.2

Throughout the 1930s Chanel's eveningwear often included garments composed of fine bands of lace interspersed with fabrics such as tulle, chiffon or velvet, in both horizontal and vertical compositions. In November 1930 *Vogue* noted, 'Chanel is doing a great deal with lace, this year. She uses it in combination with satin…, and her lace and tulle combinations are, perhaps, the most charming of all'.[32] This dress worn by Minoru, Lady Foley (see also no.22), is composed of alternating tulle and lace sections in a delicate zigzag configuration worn over a satin petticoat. Despite its impactful full-skirted silhouette the dress is incredibly lightweight, its construction exemplifying the skill of the 'flou' atelier, the section of the haute couture house that concentrates on soft-dressmaking, as opposed to tailoring, using the finest and lightest materials. **OC**

Lace was a favourite medium for eveningwear for Chanel and remained a staple of her collection throughout the 1930s. Black lace featured particularly often. In this dress of Autumn/Winter 1932, Chanel plays with the transparency of lace by edging the neckline with a semi-sheer panel tracing the line of the bust and evoking a lingerie aesthetic. A delicately scalloped hem and subtle flounce on the left hip heighten the feminine feel of the garment. The unusual, capped sleeves are held away from the shoulders by short metal boning. Writing in the French magazine *L'Illustration* in 1939, Chanel shared her thoughts on one of her favourite materials: 'I consider lace to be one of the prettiest imitations that has been made from the fantasies of nature…for me it evokes the incomparable designs that embroider the sky, the leaves and the branches of trees.'[33] **CKB**

33. DRESS

AUTUMN/WINTER 1932
SILK LACE, METAL
PATRIMOINE DE CHANEL, PARIS:
HC.AH.1932.2

Fig. 67 'This charming black lace gown is typical of the silhouette stressed by Chanel in her evening models', *The Bystander*, March 1932. Sketch by Drian

Fig. 68 Chanel gown, sketched for
Bergdorf Goodman, 1932. The
Irene Lewisohn Costume Reference
Library, The Costume Institute, The
Metropolitan Museum of Art, New York

34. DRESS

AUTUMN/WINTER 1932
COTTON VELVET
PATRIMOINE DE CHANEL, PARIS:
HC.AH.1932.3
WORN BY MADAME LUCILE DE CHAUDENAY,
NÉE LUCILE EONNET (1914–1974)

In August 1932 *The Times* reported on the new Paris fashions for winter, highlighting that, 'Cloth and cotton velvet specially made in Manchester for Chanel' was being used in her collections. As with this dress and matching gloves, the article went on to note that, 'For the evening Chanel makes long gloves of cotton velvet in the colour of a dress'.[34] Traditionally, silk velvet, a softer more draping fabric, was used for haute couture garments, with cotton velvet or velour seen as more humble materials. Once again, Chanel demonstrated how she was not afraid to subvert preconceptions of textiles to challenge the rules in her unique approach to design. **OC**

Fig. 69 Chanel gown, sketched for
Bergdorf Goodman, 1932. The
Irene Lewisohn Costume Reference
Library, The Costume Institute, The
Metropolitan Museum of Art, New York

35. DRESS

1932
SILK CREPE, SEQUINS
V&A: T.339-1960
GIVEN BY LOELIA, DUCHESS OF
WESTMINSTER

This dress elegantly balances a paired-back silhouette with lavish decoration. The simple sheath, with gored skirt cut to flare below the knee, is transformed by the all-over sequin embellishment. It is further enhanced by two trompe-l'oeil sequin bows cleverly incorporated into the flat surface, one across the bust and the other at the back of the dress, suggestively set across the bottom. In August 1934 *The Times* commented on Chanel's evening dresses, which had 'full backs with bows set low behind'.[35] This dress was worn by the Hon. Loelia, Duchess of Westminster. Born Loelia Ponsonby, she was one of the 'Bright Young Things', a young aristocratic circle who frequently featured in the newspapers of 1920s London for their parties and misbehaviour. Loelia married the Duke of Westminster in 1930, becoming his third wife right in the middle of his decade-long affair with Chanel. As might be expected, Loelia and Chanel were never close friends. However, as a lover of elegant and fashionable clothes, the Duchess was not averse to ordering garments from the celebrated couturière. **OC**

Chanel often favoured wearing an abundance of jewellery. However, with this dress she negated the need for any necklace by incorporating imitation gems into the dress itself. Sparkling paste rhinestones on the straps add a sensual element that draws the eye to the exposed shoulders and back. The unusual scoop-neck bodice with conventional shoulder straps is combined with a separate, overlaid panel finishing in a central halter-neck. Four jewelled straps adorn the shoulders and meet at the centre back. The dress is made from cream-coloured lace over a silk satin lining. The lace is embroidered with couched gilt-metal thread forming floral shapes and giving a subtle sparkle to the surface of the garment. Chanel reprised this idea of metal thread embroidery over lace in her later collections (see no.46). **CKB**

36. DRESS

AUTUMN/WINTER 1933
SILK LACE, METALLIC THREAD,
RHINESTONES
PATRIMOINE DE CHANEL, PARIS:
HC.AH.1933.1

Fig. 70 Studio Chanel, Autumn/Winter 1933. Patrimoine de CHANEL, Paris

Chanel's experimental use of textiles did not stop at jersey and tweed. In the early 1930s she popularized cotton, previously viewed as a daywear fabric, for evening dresses. She made much use of organdie, a fine, transparent cotton fabric with a stiff body to it, although she also employed other cotton fabrics. The different types of cotton weaves were described by *The New York Times*: 'Chanel has added to her famous organdies, evening gowns of cross-barred muslin and dotted Swiss. Often these are trimmed with incrustations of cotton lace or with many tiny cotton lace ruffles.'[36] For Spring/Summer 1933, the collection from which this dress comes, the press noted that Chanel was now tinting her whites with pale pink, like a soft sunset glow, highlighting a 'lovely evening frock of pale pink organdie with white flowers embroidered on it'.[37] Cotton evening dresses were intended to appeal to a younger clientele and an organdie Chanel dress from this same collection, with a very similar silhouette, appeared in the magazine *Britannia and Eve* in June 1933, recommended as 'a lovely gown for a debutante'.[38] With its soft ruffled cape-like collar, pretty neck bow and laced-up bodice, this dress embodies youthful style. **OC**

37. DRESS

SPRING/SUMMER 1933
EMBROIDERED ORGANDIE
PATRIMOINE DE CHANEL, PARIS:
HC.PE.1933.2

Left
Fig. 71 *Britannia and Eve*, 1 June 1933

Right
Fig. 72 *L'Officiel de la Mode*, March 1933

This striking evening dress from 1933 is one of Chanel's more sensual designs. The jet-black viscose rayon rep textile has a gentle sheen and is cut on the bias so that the dress gently skims the curves of the body. Chanel creates interest at the neckline with a cut-out design and delicately draped off-the-shoulder short sleeves. At the rear, an almost entirely bare back is revealed with a dramatic deep 'V' opening, drawing the eye downward to overlapping pattern pieces arranged on the backside. A ruffled trim at the hem demonstrates the powerful impact of the stark contrast of black and white so associated with Chanel. The sleek silhouette and sex appeal of this dress echo the costumes designed by Chanel for Hollywood film stars Gloria Swanson and Ina Claire in *Tonight or Never* (1931) and *The Greeks Had a Word for Them* (1932), respectively (see p.36 and fig.27). **CKB**

38. DRESS

AUTUMN/WINTER 1933
RAYON REP, SILK ORGANZA
PATRIMOINE DE CHANEL, PARIS:
HC.AH.1933.2

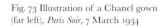
Fig. 73 Illustration of a Chanel gown (far left), *Paris Soir*, 7 March 1934

39. DRESS

1935
PRINTED SILK ORGANZA
PATRIMOINE DE CHANEL, PARIS:
HC.INC.1935.3

Fig. 74 Chanel dress of printed chiffon
on the cover of *Modes et Travaux*,
August 1935

Dix-septième Année. — N° 375   1ᵉʳ Août 1935

Modes *et* Travaux

France et Colonies: 4 francs   EDITIONS EDOUARD BOUCHERIT   10, Rue de la Pépinière, Paris

When creating this evening dress of 1935, Chanel aligned each pattern piece carefully on the silk organza to ensure a perfectly symmetrical placement of the floral print. Printed fabrics were a key part of both Chanel's daywear and evening ensembles in the 1920s and '30s, many of which had been designed and produced in her own textile factories (see p.31). Chanel often favoured floral patterns and utilized these printed motifs further by employing an unusual appliqué technique. Described in 1930 by Lois Long of the *New Yorker* as the 'new Chanel trick',[39] the individual floral motifs in a print were cut out and the edges carefully hand-finished. These printed chiffon flowers were then re-applied as three-dimensional decoration to particular elements, sometimes adorning the hem, the neckline or emphasizing the lines of the dress. The technique was used repeatedly by Chanel in the late 1920s and '30s (see nos 25 and 26). Referencing Chanel's appliqué, the *Washington Sunday Star* declared that 'her Summer evening gowns of flowered chiffon are works of art', adding that they required 'meticulous workmanship'.[40] The technique is seen here on the back of the dress, demarcating where the skirt begins to flare out at the rear, and on the sleeves, giving added volume to the ruffled edges. This design focus is demonstrated in the illustration on the cover of the French magazine *Modes et Travaux*. **CKB**

40. DRESS

AUTUMN/WINTER 1937
LACE, TULLE, SILK VELVET
PATRIMOINE DE CHANEL, PARIS:
HC.AH.1937.1

In 1936 *The New York Times* noted regarding the Parisian vogue for lace evening dresses that, 'this naturally makes one think of Chanel, who does that sort of thing better than anybody. She handles delicate lace with frosty precision, fitting it like a skin where it should fit but allowing it to spray out like a cloud to balance the composition'.[41] This dress, made a year later, with its horizontal banding of velvet and lace, perfectly expresses this expertise, deftly balancing a heavier fabric with a lightweight one. Velvet ribbon is used for the shoulder straps and the bodice incorporates graded ribbon banding crossed over at the waist to create a narrow sash tied at the back. Highlighting one of the many crucial ancillary trades of the haute couture industry, *The Times* reported in November 1937 that a number of couturiers had used ribbons in their collections and 'these points show that the efforts that have been made by the Centre du Ruban [Ribbon Centre] to bring ribbon into fashion have been successful'.[42] This dress displays intricate details and decorative elements contained within a very simple silhouette, a hallmark of Chanel's design expertise. **OC**

Fig. 75 Chanel gown in *L'Art et la Mode*, November 1937. Photograph by Studio Dorvyne

This afternoon dress is made from alternating panels of delicate machine-made lace and tulle, the translucent fabrics and gracefully scalloped neckline giving the garment a lingerie feel. The combination of lace and other sheer fabrics was a Chanel signature during the 1930s. The dress originally had a large satin bow attached at the waist and a delicate tulle and lace cape designed to be draped around the shoulders, fixed at one side with a brooch. Chanel often paired her dresses with capes and fichus, as described by *The Times*: 'triangular scarves of tulle and chiffon edged with lace go with picture-frocks'.[43] The dress was worn by Fern Bedaux at the wedding of the Duke of Windsor and Wallis Simpson in June 1937. The ceremony took place at the home of Fern and Charles Bedaux, the Château de Candé, in the Loire Valley. Charles Bedaux, a wealthy French-American industrial consultant, was arrested in Algiers in 1944 and transported to America where he was charged with treason for collaboration with Nazi forces. **SW**

41. DRESS

SPRING/SUMMER 1937
SILK LACE, TULLE
V&A: T.748 TO B-1972
BEQUEATHED BY MRS FERN BEDAUX

Fig. 76 The Duke and Duchess of Windsor and guests on their wedding day, among them Fern Bedaux wearing a gown by Chanel (far right), Château de Candé, Monts, 3 June 1937

Botanical forms appear regularly in Chanel's jewellery from the 1930s. Particularly popular were her floral necklaces and brooches, executed by the Parisian jewellery atelier Maison Gripoix (see p.35). Individual petals were created using the firm's own specialist *pâte de verre* technique and then assembled to produce hyperreal, three-dimensional flowers. Translucent green leaves gave a luscious finishing touch. Chanel herself was pictured wearing one of these floral designs on the cover of the French magazine *Le Crapouillot* in April 1938. **CKB**

42. BROOCH

1937
GILT METAL AND GLASS PASTE
PATRIMOINE DE CHANEL, PARIS:
ACC.HC.INC.1937.2

MENSUEL   Avril 1938   4 fr.

CRAPOUILLOT
ARTS - LETTRES - SPECTACLES

Portrait de Mademoiselle Chanel, par VERTÈS
(Exposition à la Galerie de l'Elysée)

Fig. 77 Gabrielle Chanel wearing a necklace of floral forms, *Le Crapouillot*, April 1938. Illustration by Marcel Vertès

43. SUIT

AUTUMN/WINTER 1937
SILK TULLE, SEQUINS, CHIFFON, LACE
V&A: T.88 TO B-1974
GIVEN BY MRS DIANA VREELAND

Fashion editor Diana Vreeland was a loyal Chanel client. She wore this sequinned trouser suit for entertaining at home in the winter of 1937–8. Reports on the Paris collections noted that it was a season of 'gorgeous evening styles…with sequins and jewelled embroidery'.[44] The lightest of tulle grounds supports the embroidered sequins of this ensemble so that the unstructured suit with bolero jacket and flowing pleat-front trousers adheres to Chanel's diktat of clothes being comfortable while also chic. She provided an intriguing contrast by pairing the hard shiny glamour of the suit with a light ethereal frill-neck blouse. Although the couturière advocated trousers for casual wear and sportswear, this outfit is something of an anomaly as trousers did not feature regularly in her collections until the 1960s. In later life Vreeland wrote fondly of her Chanel clothes from this period. **OC**

Extravagant eveningwear such as this full-length, sequinned net dress and cape, from 1937, was a staple of Chanel's creative output during the 1930s. The combination of glistening black sequins and scarlet satin is striking. The dress is made of black net entirely covered with overlapping black sequins and features a sleeveless bodice with straps, constructed over a boned foundation panel at the waist. A satin double sash encircles the waist, flowing into matching panels inset into the skirt. The short, semi-circular cape has been lined with the same scarlet satin. This red-and-black colour scheme, combined with the sash and shoulder cape, evokes a Catholic cardinal's cassock and mozzetta or pellegrina cape. The ensemble was worn by American socialite Mrs Leo d'Erlanger, formerly Miss Edwina Prue. She featured regularly in fashion and society magazines in the 1930s, including American *Vogue, Tatler* and *The Sketch*, and was celebrated for her sense of style and beauty. **SW**

44. DRESS

AUTUMN/WINTER 1937
SILK SATIN, NET, SEQUINS
V&A: T.87&A−1974
GIVEN BY MRS LEO D'ERLANGER

Fig. 78 Sketch of a Chanel evening gown, August 1937. Berley Collection, Fashion Institute of Technology, New York

45. DRESS

SPRING/SUMMER 1939
GROSGRAIN, SILK CHIFFON
V&A: T.32–1978

Fig. 79 Sketch of a Chanel evening
dress, Spring/Summer 1939. The
Irene Lewisohn Costume Reference
Library, The Costume Institute, The
Metropolitan Museum of Art,
New York

In February 1939 *The New York Times*, reporting on Chanel's recent Spring/Summer collection, highlighted her eveningwear, noting: 'Sixteenth century French history has inspired an outstanding formal evening group. The styles of this period are translated into tight grosgrain corselets with ripply basques and nude modern décolletages with full, filmy skirts in contrasting mousseline or lace.'[45] While it was unusual in the early years of her career for Chanel to make overt historic references, by the mid-1930s she was not afraid to incorporate and reinterpret elements associated with previous periods. By the end of the decade her collections began to evolve with a focus on tighter waistlines and longer hemlines. This red dress combines a long floating chiffon skirt, gathered in at the waist, with a grosgrain bodice. The bodice is cleverly edged with its own fabric selvedge, and while the original version of the dress was strapless, this particular garment has additional shoulder straps also fashioned from the selvedge. This collection was noted for its patriotic use of red, white and blue, but although appearing to represent these colours, the selvedge is actually in a red, white and black stripe. The bodice has light vertical boning sewn into the internal seams. It is fastened at the front with concealed hooks and eyes. Three horizontal tucks either side of the opening add shaping to the bust. The hem of the bodice has tabs that are sewn into the skirt on one side, emphasizing the narrowness of the waist and giving a flared effect over the hips. The dress was originally shown with an impressive suite of Chanel's red and green cabochon costume jewellery comprising a bejewelled choker, bracelet and earrings. **OC**

While Chanel's work is often viewed in opposition to the style of Dior's 'New Look', she was very aware of the prevailing (and popular) fashionable silhouette when she relaunched her label in 1954. In fact, her final collections of the 1930s had predicted this line with cinched-in waists and full skirts, so she had experience of creating the silhouette. Yet, in Chanel's hands the bodice had a much less constricting internal construction than many of the contemporary garments of similar style. Chanel was not afraid to continually reference her own rich history of design, and the effect of this skirt with alternating vertical bands of tulle and applied lace recalls the style of an earlier Chanel gown of 1937 (see no.41) in the V&A collection. **OC**

46. DRESS

SPRING/SUMMER 1954
SILK, TULLE, SILK LACE, METAL
PATRIMOINE DE CHANEL, PARIS:
HC.PE.1954.4

Fig. 80 A dress from Chanel's Spring/ Summer 1954 return collection, *Le nouveau fémina*, March 1954. Photograph by Lionel Kazan (Studio Chevalier)

In September 1954 Chanel showed her second collection after more than 15 years away from fashion. Chanel's designs for the autumn saw her build on the foundations of the previous season and hone her individual interpretation of the prevailing trends (see p.48). This demure black velvet dress with its defined waist and full skirt undoubtedly evokes Dior's 'New Look' silhouette while also, arguably, still being true to Chanel's enduring design approach. It is based on an adaptable, utilitarian garment – the shirt dress – presented with restrained adornment and styled simply with a long string of pearls and rhinestones, as illustrated by René Gruau. Three-quarter-length sleeves and a wide, open collar give a relaxed touch. Interestingly, it was reportedly the only outfit of the collection with which Chanel's characteristic string of pearls was worn.[46] Journalists noted that many of Chanel's eveningwear designs for the season featured covered arms, high necklines and ankle-length skirts.[47] This ensemble belonged to Oona O'Neill Chaplin, wife of Charlie Chaplin. **CKB**

47. DRESS

AUTUMN/WINTER 1954
SILK VELVET
PATRIMOINE DE CHANEL, PARIS:
HC.AH.1954.3

Fig. 81 Chanel evening dress,
American *Vogue*, December 1954.
Illustration by René Gruau

Chanel news: complete evening coverage

Just two of the dinner-evening dresses from Chanel's new collection—but they tell everything
about her new love of coverage: arms are sleeved, necklines high,
skirts flared (from the hipbone) to the ankle—or almost.

132

In 1955 *Vogue* reported from the Paris collections on 'a suit that is a fashion-law unto itself – that is to say a Chanel suit. It is one of the few fitted to the waist suits in Paris'.[48] Although Chanel was later known for the boxy cut of her jackets, the period of her relaunch saw her acknowledging the prevailing line of fashion, albeit in her own style as this fitted jacket demonstrates. The rich burgundy tweed of the suit is offset by a deep navy jersey facing on the lapels and cuffs and a trim on the pockets and buttons. In place of a blouse is a charming fitted jersey jumper with buttoned waistline and a small jersey bow at the neck. The suit is one of a number of pieces donated to the V&A from the wardrobe of the model Anne Gunning, later Lady Nutting. **OC**

48. SUIT

*c.*1955
WOOL TWEED, JERSEY
V&A: T.123–1990
GIVEN BY SIR ANTHONY NUTTING IN
MEMORY OF ANNE, LADY NUTTING

When Chanel relaunched her label in 1954, in order to further simplify her formula for dressing, she decided to create a bag that would be adaptable to all eventualities. With external quilting inspired by equestrian equipment, the bag was offered in lambskin, jersey or silk. Wishing to dispense with the bother of holding a bag in her hand, Chanel ensured that the bag incorporated a strengthened chain shoulder strap, which also gave the decorative effect of jewellery. Launched in February 1955, in keeping with her fondness for numeric titles she named it the 2.55 handbag. **OC**

49. HANDBAG

1955–71
LEATHER, METAL
PATRIMOINE DE CHANEL, PARIS:
ACC.HC.INC.1954–1971.3

Fig. 82 Model Shauna Trabert,
Life magazine, September 1961.
Photograph by Paul Schutzer

50. COCKTAIL DRESS

AUTUMN/WINTER 1956
SILK, LACE, SATIN
V&A: T.131–1990
GIVEN BY SIR ANTHONY NUTTING, IN
MEMORY OF ANNE, LADY NUTTING

Cocktail and evening dresses of black or white lace featured regularly in Chanel's collections during the 1950s and '60s. This strapless, form-fitting example from 1956 is made of black lace over silk, constructed over a boned foundation. Its trumpet-shaped skirt flares to a triple flounce at the hem that is supported by a layered petticoat heavily stiffened with a deep band of black net. Reporting on the collection for the British press, journalist Hazel Hackett picked out this dress, commenting that 'one swathed black lace dress had a flamenco flavour with its bunch of low-set flounces'.[49] With its boned construction and stiffened petticoat, it is a key example of Chanel's experimentation with structure and is a world away from her signature draping bias-cut and free-flowing dresses of the 1930s. Its slender, flared shape represents Chanel's own take on the 1950s silhouette that typically saw either the pencil skirt or voluminous full skirt in most evening dresses of the time. **SW**

Fig. 83 Lace dress from Chanel's Autumn/Winter 1956 collection, *L'Officiel de la couture et de la Mode de Paris*, December 1956. Photograph by Philippe Pottier

In 1957 Chanel chose Massaro, a shoemaker based on the prestigious rue de la Paix, to develop the ultimate Chanel shoe. As always, she designed to suit her own wardrobe. She selected a beige leather to match her skin tone, giving the appearance of an elongated leg. A small black toecap provided a tiny punctuation over the toes that visually shortened the foot and protected the paler leather from the dirt of the street. Chanel would introduce three further toecap options: in brown, navy and, for eveningwear, gold. **OC**

51. SHOE

1960–2
LEATHER, SILK SATIN
PATRIMOINE DE CHANEL, PARIS:
ACC.HC.INC.1960–1962.1

Fig. 84 Model Alexandra (born Veronika Haak), French *Vogue*, September 1964. Photograph by Helmut Newton

52. SUIT

SPRING/SUMMER 1959
WOOL, PRINTED SILK, METAL
V&A: T.11 TO B-1971
GIVEN BY THE EDUCATIONAL FOUNDATION
FOR THE FASHION INDUSTRIES,
NEW YORK

Paris haute couture maintained an undeniable pull for the international follower of fashion in the 1950s. Hollywood actors were among those making frequent trips to select salons in the French capital to acquire the latest styles for their red-carpet-worthy wardrobes. This classic suit was ordered by American actor Lauren Bacall (1924–2014) from Chanel's Spring/Summer 1959 collection. Bacall was photographed wearing it in July 1959 at London Airport (now Heathrow), alongside her children, about to board a plane to Biarritz for their family holiday. The expectation for women in the public eye to be immaculately well-presented and photo-ready at any moment meant that even on personal errands Hollywood's stars had to live up to their glamorous personas. Chanel's coveted suits proved to be the outfit of choice for many, being comfortable and chic in equal measure. They appear to have been a favourite of Bacall's when she was travelling in this period: she was photographed at the same airport just two months earlier, on return from shooting her latest film, wearing a similar Chanel suit in a checked tweed.

The slim, straight-cut jacket with simple stand collar created a sleek silhouette on Bacall. The vertical opening of the flap pockets was a point of difference from other Chanel suits that season. Subtle beige undertones running through the rose-pink tweed complement the sleeveless printed silk blouse. Bacall wore it with a flower in her top buttonhole and a pair of white gloves. **CKB**

Fig. 85 Lauren Bacall wearing a
Chanel suit, with her children Stephen
and Leslie, London Airport, 1959

53. SUIT

SPRING/SUMMER 1960
WOOL, PRINTED SILK
V&A: T.74:1 TO 3–2023
GIVEN BY CHANEL

This suit's unusual combination of a bold check in pink, heather and brown and a rose-patterned chiné silk creates a lively juxtaposition. The sympathetic hues of the fabrics bring together the otherwise contrasting linear check with the soft, organic floral print. The matching silk blouse is sleeveless but, characteristically, Chanel has added cuffs of the floral silk onto the jacket to create the illusion of a long-sleeved blouse underneath.

French singer and actor Juliette Gréco (1927–2020) ordered a version of this vibrant suit from Chanel's Spring/Summer 1960 collection. Known for her style, Gréco was a regular at Chanel's salons and was frequently photographed wearing Chanel suits and evening dresses in the press throughout the 1960s. She also wore Chanel on-screen in films such as *Where the Truth Lies* (1962), including a cream tweed suit featuring the same V-shaped appliqué detailing on the pockets as this 1960 suit. **CKB**

Fig. 86 Jean-Marc Bory and Juliette
Gréco in *Where the Truth Lies*, 1962

54. SUIT

SPRING/SUMMER 1960
SILK TWILL, GROSGRAIN
PATRIMOINE DE CHANEL, PARIS:
HC.PE.1960.6

A youthful summer iteration of the classic Chanel suit, a version of this lightweight silk twill suit was worn by celebrated French actress Jeanne Moreau at Cannes Film Festival in 1960, the year she won the Best Actress Award for *Seven Days…Seven Nights*. The printed silk is edged with grosgrain ribbon trims in blue and red, which tie in a statement bow at the neckline. From the very start of her career, Chanel appreciated the custom of well-known actresses and Moreau was an important client of the House. The couturière created her costumes for several films, including *The Lovers* (1958), and the two often spent time together in Chanel's apartment at 31 rue Cambon. **OC**

Fig. 87 Jean-Paul Belmondo and Jeanne Moreau at Cannes Film Festival, 20 May 1960

55. SUIT

SPRING/SUMMER 1961
WOOL, SILK
V&A: T.128–1990
GIVEN BY SIR ANTHONY NUTTING, IN
MEMORY OF ANNE, LADY NUTTING

Chanel's love of wool tweed continued throughout her long career, however the muted tones that she favoured to line her tweed ensembles in the 1920s and '30s were replaced by bold, hot colours in the post-war period. This grey-and-white bouclé wool tweed coat dress features a bright pink quilted silk lining. The same pink silk is used to face the collar and edge the bouclé wool buttons. The coat dress is part of a collection of Chanel garments worn by leading 1950s model Anne Gunning and given to the V&A by her husband, Sir Anthony Nutting, in her memory. It is from the Spring/Summer 1961 collection, the same year that Gunning married Sir Anthony.

Gunning was originally a house model for Irish designer Sybil Connolly and went on to become a top photographic model of the 1950s, gaining global recognition after appearing on the cover of *Life* magazine in August 1953. Speaking of her hesitancy to model in fashion shows she said, 'That sea of faces glaring at me was too daunting. Chanel asked me to model a collection for her, but I knew I couldn't do it…I realize now I should have done it. I might have got all my Chanel suits for nothing if I had!'[50] **SW**

Chanel's experimentation with vibrant colour for her classic tailored suits can be seen in this lilac wool mohair tweed suit from Autumn/Winter 1964. Beneath the jacket, a dress takes the appearance of a separate blouse and skirt. The loosely woven tweed, trademarked Kanimura, was made by London-based textile manufacturer Ascher Ltd. Ascher gained a reputation for developing and supplying a new range of mohair mix fabrics to Paris couture in the late 1950s and '60s. The material is extremely lightweight compared with traditional wool tweed, in line with Chanel's design philosophy that clothes should be elegant, comfortable and easy to move in. The jacket is lined with a cream silk printed with mauve and brown irises, which also forms the fabric of the sleeveless dress bodice and neck bow, creating a unified look. The skirt is lined in the same silk, a luxurious detail of which only the wearer would have been aware. The jacket has faux blouse sleeves below the wool cuff, giving the appearance of a long-sleeved blouse underneath.

This same suit design featured in French and British *Vogue* in May 1964, which celebrated its 'soft and relaxed tailoring' and 'precise detailing'.[51] The suit retailed at British chain-store Wallis, which specialized in ready-to-wear copies of Chanel designs, offered at significantly lower prices than the original couture pieces. **SW**

56. SUIT

SPRING/SUMMER 1964
WOOL, PRINTED SILK GAUZE
V&A: T.90 TO C–1974
GIVEN BY BARONESS ALAIN DE ROTHSCHILD

Fig. 88 Chanel suits, Spring/Summer 1964 collection, *Jours de France*, February 1964. Photograph by Nicolas Tikhomiroff

57. NECKLACE

AUTUMN/WINTER 1938
GILT METAL, GLASS PASTE, GLASS BEADS,
IMITATION PEARLS
PATRIMOINE DE CHANEL, PARIS:
ACC.HC.AH.1938.3

58. GROUP OF JEWELLERY

NECKLACE
CHANEL DESIGN MADE BY
ROBERT GOOSSENS
1960S
GILT METAL, MOTHER-OF-PEARL
V&A: M.42–1990

NECKLACE
SPRING/SUMMER 1959
GILT METAL, MOTHER-OF-PEARL, GLASS
V&A: M.43–1990

BROOCH
CHANEL DESIGN MADE BY
ROBERT GOOSSENS
1960S
GILT METAL, MOTHER-OF-PEARL, GLASS
V&A: M.40–1990

BROOCH OR PENDANT
CHANEL DESIGN MADE BY
ROBERT GOOSSENS
SPRING/SUMMER 1957
GILT METAL, MOTHER-OF-PEARL, GLASS
V&A: M.39–1990

ALL OBJECTS GIVEN BY SIR ANTHONY
NUTTING, IN MEMORY OF ANNE,
LADY NUTTING

When Chanel returned to fashion in 1954, she revived her line of costume jewellery, drawing on many of the themes and styles she had employed in the 1930s. Several of Chanel's post-war designs were created by Robert Goossens (see p.53).[52] A trained goldsmith, through an apprenticeship at Lefebvre and stints working at a range of specialist ateliers in Paris, Goossens had learnt techniques not just for metal but also leather, wood, glass, ivory, shell and enamel, all of which went on to inform his inventive and adaptable approach to jewellery creation. His years of training resulted in a great versatility of skill in the art of metalwork. He combined these specialist techniques in his jewellery in gloriously varied combinations. His studies of historical jewellery chimed well with Chanel's own design language and together they drew inspiration from the bejewelled antiques they saw in museums and books. Occasionally, Chanel asked Goossens to copy an ancient pendant but more often the historical artefacts served as muses from which to create something new.[53] As described by one of her biographers, Marcel Haedrich, Chanel would pick out the selection of gems and arrange them herself, presenting her designs for Goossens to interpret and manifest.[54] Before the debut showing of her collections, Chanel carefully selected pieces to accompany each look worn by her models, and according to Goossens, 'choosing pieces to go with the colour of their eyes or the colour of their hair. She was a colourist and that was how she saw things.'[55] **CKB**

A two-tone wool braid trim in navy and red adorns the collar, centre front opening, hem, cuffs and pocket openings of this classic Chanel suit. The seemingly simple decoration gives a striking and surprising effect, creating graphic interest and defining the cut of the jacket. This ensemble has all the hallmarks of the quintessential post-war Chanel suit: the straight, cardigan-cut jacket, simple skirt, textured tweed and false shirt cuffs (see pp.49–50). From a distance, the jacket appears to be made from a plain cream wool, but closer inspection reveals a tweed with a complex fabric structure with yarns of different weights that create texture and movement on the surface. This particular model was perhaps a personal favourite of Chanel herself as she was often photographed wearing a suit of a similar style. In 1964, *New York Times* reporter Joseph Barry described Chanel wearing a suit with a 'boxy cardigan jacket' in 'soft beige tweed trimmed with bright red and dark blue braid', calling it 'her favourite suit of the moment' and noting that she had not only been wearing it 'steadily' for 10 months, but also that she had reproduced the same design, two years after its debut, in her latest collection.[56] Barry observed how the suit moved with her 'as limberly as a leopard's own leopard skin'. **CKB**

59. SUIT

AUTUMN/WINTER 1964
WOOL, WOOL BRAID, SILK
PATRIMOINE DE CHANEL, PARIS:
HC.AH.1964.12

Fig. 89 Gabrielle Chanel attends the Prix de Diane at the Chantilly Racecourse, wearing one of her favourite suits, June 1964. Photograph by Shahrokh Hatami

For spring 1966 Chanel chose to cut her suits closer to the body, with *Vogue* noting 'her beautiful sleeves are narrower, higher; armholes smaller. In short, completely contemporary…Yet they convey, as always, the essence of Chanel's own fashion thinking – discretion plus dash.'[57] The tweed of this suit is a unique cotton and wool mix neutral ground with the black-and-white selvedge used as a finish on the edging of the jacket, the pockets, cuffs and the opening of the wrap-around-style skirt. Unusually, the varied stripes are not woven into the fabric but have been applied afterwards, printed with tints of orange, red and pink combined to produce the irregular striped decoration. **OC**

60. SUIT

SPRING/SUMMER 1966
WOOL, COTTON
PATRIMOINE DE CHANEL, PARIS:
HC.PE.1966.7

Fig. 90 Models Monica Siwers
and Vanja Befrits wearing Chanel
suits, February 1966. Photograph
by Shahrokh Hatami

Raspberry pink and shimmering metallic orange have been paired for striking effect in this bouclé wool cocktail suit from Autumn/Winter 1961. It is a rare example of Chanel's first use of Lurex to line and trim her classic tailored suits and create a look that moved seamlessly from day into eveningwear. The printed silk and Lurex fabric of the blouse, jacket lining, cuffs and pocket flaps is called Mustafa by Lyon-based textile manufacturer Bucol. Chanel's choice of cloth represents her continued love affair with luxurious, metallic fabrics such as lamé and Lurex that had often appeared in her eveningwear, and from the mid-1950s, and particularly in the 1960s, increasingly featured in her cocktail and evening suits.

This suit design received extensive press coverage and was seen on the cover of both *Elle* magazine on 25 August 1961 and American *Vogue* on 1 October 1961, accessorized with Chanel's signature heavy gold chain and brooch. *Vogue* lauded the design as 'Chanel at peak form – which means, for many American women, a look that's simultaneously reliable as a Rolls and as whizz-bang exciting as a souped-up racer.'[58] **SW**

61. COCKTAIL SUIT

AUTUMN/WINTER 1961
WOOL, LUREX, SILK, GILT METAL
PATRIMOINE DE CHANEL, PARIS:
HC.AH.1961.4

VOGUE

60¢
Oct. 1

- **PLAN FOR A WARDROBE:**
  WHAT TO BUY, WHAT TO SKIP
  Quick review of
  the best looks
  you could choose
  in fashion now

- **FOUR NEW PARIS COIFFURES**

- **A SMALL SENSATION: THE NEW FUR BIT**

- **YOUNG-MONEY CLOTHES-BULLETIN**

- **"TAKE NO FOR AN ANSWER"**
  By Joan Didion

- **ARTICLES BY Osbert Sitwell**
  Elinor Goulding Smith
  Pamela Hansford Johnson
  George Bradshaw

Fig. 91 Chanel's tweed and lamé suit
on the cover of American *Vogue*,
1 October 1961. Photograph by
Irving Penn

62. SUIT

SPRING/SUMMER 1962
SILK LAMÉ BROCADE
PATRIMOINE DE CHANEL, PARIS:
HC.PE.1962.14

Following the success of Chanel's day suits in the 1950s (see pp.49–52), she soon adapted the style for eveningwear. Maintaining the ease of wear and smartness of her day suits, for her cocktail suits she sourced a plethora of richly decorative fabrics such as gold and silver lamés, textured weaves and intricately patterned silks. These sparkling fabrics, for which Chanel particularly favoured golden hues, evoked the glittering beads and sequins of her eveningwear in the 1920s and '30s. The chic evening ensembles usually comprised a jacket, blouse and skirt combination or a neat cocktail dress with matching jacket, as in this example from 1962. The surface of the suit is covered entirely in a woven three-dimensional foliate pattern. The filigree gold-coloured buttons blend in so that the all-over pattern is punctuated only by the flash of a red silk binding on the pocket openings. These bursts of crimson are repeated on the neck and waistline of the cocktail dress underneath, as well as in the lining of both garments. **CKB**

63. DRESS

1961
SILK CHIFFON, SILK TAFFETA
V&A: S.1645–2015
GIVEN BY THE BRITISH FILM INSTITUTE

In 1961 Chanel was invited to provide the costumes for the character known only as 'A', played by Delphine Seyrig, in Alain Resnais's unconventional New Wave film *Last Year at Marienbad*. Chanel drew on pieces from her haute couture collections, creating ensembles that were contemporary and classic in equal measure. This dress, one of several Chanel creations worn by Seyrig in the film, is in plain black chiffon decorated with 12 rows of gathered ruffles. The back of the dress features a dramatic black taffeta bow. The fashionable appeal of the film lingered for some time: in her coverage of Chanel's Autumn/Winter collection of 1964, journalist Nathalie Pernikoff described a 'type of sheer chiffon or organdie coat which she originally designed for the film *Last Year at Marienbad*, and which has remained a top fashion ever since'.[59] **CKB**

Fig. 92 Delphine Seyrig in *Last Year at Marienbad*, 1961

Throughout her career, Chanel favoured metallic fabrics such as lamés for eveningwear. In the 1950s and '60s, thanks to synthetic fibres, these fabrics became more flexible. From 1958 she worked closely with the Lyon-based textile manufacturer Bucol, choosing its most innovative fabrics: Toutaluma, Beldor and Bichedor – their names evoke the brilliance of the precious metal that they imitate. These glistening textiles were woven in silk and Lurex, or made with newly developed fibres such as Rhodia, Dralon or Orlon combined with polyester threads and tapes covered with a metallic layer. Chanel used these fabrics not only for eveningwear but also for the blouses that accompanied her day suits. For this dress, Chanel selected a cloqué, a fabric whose complex woven structure produces a three-dimensional relief effect. Cloqués are practical as they do not crease and offer structure while remaining very lightweight. Here, the balance of the silhouette plays between a fitted bodice defining the bust, and a full skirt created with generous pleats beginning slightly below the natural waistline. **VB**

64. DRESS

AUTUMN/WINTER 1961
CLOQUÉ LAMÉ
PALAIS GALLIERA, PARIS: 1977.20.3
GIVEN BY CHANEL

Elizabeth Taylor was a regular client at the House of Chanel during the 1960s. Often photographed wearing a Chanel suit, Taylor also favoured Chanel's more experimental eveningwear. This dress comprises a bodice covered entirely in strips of silver lamé, stitched in a zigzag pattern across the body (see a similar technique used in the day dress, no.68). The zigzag motif also appears in horizontal form along the hem of the bodice. A skirt of gathered grey organza, printed with a smoky circular pattern, floats on top of an underskirt of silver lamé. The dress is worn with a full-length hooded cape of the same transparent printed organza, tied with ribbon at the neck. The ensemble reveals Chanel's continued interest in experimenting with novel materials and printed fabrics. Taylor wore a similar dress to a royal performance of *The Taming of the Shrew* at the Odeon Theatre in London in 1967, where she and her husband Richard Burton were photographed talking with Princess Margaret. **CKB**

65. DRESS AND CAPE

SPRING/SUMMER 1967
ORGANZA, LAMÉ
PATRIMOINE DE CHANEL, PARIS:
HC.PE.1967.4

Fig. 93 Richard Burton, Elizabeth Taylor and Princess Margaret attend a royal performance of *The Taming of the Shrew*, Odeon Theatre, London, 1967

This youthful cocktail dress from Chanel's Autumn/
Winter 1967 collection demonstrates how the designer
reprised forms and motifs from her earlier creations and
adapted and updated them for a new generation. Tiered
skirts can be seen in many of Chanel's evening dresses
of the 1930s. The stepped silhouette of the skirt of this
dress reinterprets this technique, and translates it into
the style of the 1960s. Rather than the supple silk satins
and chiffons of her 1930s designs, here Chanel chooses
a stiff lamé that gives structure to the layered tiers of the
skirt. A check pattern, arranged diagonally, enhances the
geometric appearance. **CKB**

66. DRESS

AUTUMN/WINTER 1967
SILK, LAMÉ
PATRIMOINE DE CHANEL, PARIS:
HC.AH.1967.6

Fig. 94 Photograph and fabric
swatches from Chanel's Autumn/
Winter 1967 collection. Patrimoine
de CHANEL, Paris

If one look could capture Chanel's continued fashion relevance in 1968, it would arguably be this ensemble, which drew much press attention and appealed to a young clientele. It was worn by models of the moment Marisa Berenson in *Vogue* and Lauren Hutton in a Chanel N°5 advertisement. The suit also featured in an *Elle* magazine shoot photographed by Helmut Newton. Describing the outfit in the fashion hyperbole of the time, *Vogue* referred to the fact that it had been inspired by Indian dress, titling the look a 'Lamé Indian tunic' and likening it to something that might have been worn by a 'young Rajput prince'.[60] This language reflects the attitude of western fashion in this period (and in decades to come), when global cultures were liberally referenced as sources of inspiration without relevant context or acknowledgement of original creators. **OC**

CHANEL

67. SUIT

AUTUMN/WINTER 1968
SILK LAMÉ BROCADE
PATRIMOINE DE CHANEL, PARIS:
HC.AH.1968.5

Fig. 95 Lauren Hutton in an advertisement for Chanel N°5, 1968

Designed as part of an ensemble with a fur-lined double-breasted coat and matching toque hat, this brightly coloured winter dress is made from an unusual fabric that is neither knitted nor woven. The textile consists of multicoloured woollen threads, placed onto a ground fabric in a zigzag pattern then stitched over in vertical lines to secure them: a technique known as couching. The neckline and sleeve hems are edged with a simple blanket stitch, which gives a craft-like finish to the garment. In the design of this dress Chanel also plays with her classic lining technique, often found inside her suit jackets. Here, the usual vertical bands of stitching that give a quilted effect are subverted to sit in horizontal rows visible on the outer side of the garment where they hit the points of the zigzags. This dress, purported to have come from Chanel's own wardrobe, was sold at Christie's auction house in 1978 (see p.278). **OC**

(see p.278)

68. DRESS

AUTUMN/WINTER 1969
WOOL, SILK
V&A: T.375−2009

Fig. 96 Gabrielle Chanel used this characterful zigzag couched wool textile for several models in her Autumn/Winter 1969 collection. Patrimoine de CHANEL, Paris

Many photographs document Chanel's personal adoption of trousers, which she tended to wear in more informal settings such as when enjoying countryside pursuits, for sailing or at the beach, relaxing at her villa in the south of France, or in the guise of evening pyjamas to be worn when entertaining at home. This last iteration was a style that she translated into her couture collections during the 1930s. For her evening pyjamas Chanel favoured luxurious satins or chiffons, although she occasionally experimented with embellished textiles (see no.43). They usually consisted of generously draped, wide-legged trousers and a loose blouse or tunic top in a matching fabric. Chanel reprised this idea in the late 1960s, releasing what *Vogue* enthusiastically referred to as Chanel's 'famous new dinner pyjamas'.[61] While her trousered evening ensembles of this period were far more tailored than her fluid designs of the 1930s, they maintained a relaxed fit by echoing the cardigan-cut jacket of her day suits. Generally made from glistening brocades and lamés, they often featured an asymmetric opening to the jacket, three-quarter-length sleeves and cropped, straight-legged or lightly flared trousers. The plain black bouclé wool jersey of this suit has a much more subdued feel. Chanel has stripped back and refined her design to the bare essentials: an asymmetric opening, three plain buttons and large patch pockets on each hip are the only decoration. The result is a timeless garment that would be easy to wear, comfortable and undeniably chic. Chanel styled the suit with an array of long necklaces. **CKB**

69. TROUSER SUIT

AUTUMN/WINTER 1969
BOUCLÉ WOOL JERSEY
PATRIMOINE DE CHANEL, PARIS:
HC.AH.1969.4

Fig. 97 Model Maija Porkka poses in a wool trouser suit from Chanel's Autumn/Winter 1969 collection. Patrimoine de CHANEL, Paris

The unceasing popularity of Chanel's suits did not deter her creativity or ability to stay in tune with changing fashion trends. Each season she updated her formula in line with the fashion Zeitgeist, offering fresh colours and fabrics, and tweaks to the silhouette and decoration. The focus on wearability and movement, however, did not change. In this ensemble, the classic characteristics of a Chanel suit have been melded with on-trend details that welcomed in a new decade. A simple, cream linen-look textile contrasts with playful elements in the cut and construction. The knee-length skirt features a series of box pleats that run halfway up the thigh, promising a pleasing movement and flair when the wearer walked. These pleats are reflected in the peplum jacket, where they emerge from the belted waist. Echoing the simplicity of the fabric, Chanel chose to finish the outfit with unadorned, flat-faced, round buttons. **CKB**

70. SUIT

SPRING/SUMMER 1969
LINEN, MERCERISED COTTON, SILK
V&A: T.159:1 TO 2–1998

Fig. 98 Look No.21 from Chanel's Spring/
Summer 1969 collection. Patrimoine de
CHANEL, Paris

71. ENSEMBLE

SPRING/SUMMER 1970
WOOL AND LUREX CROCHET, METAL,
GLASS
PALAIS GALLIERA, PARIS: 1972.75.5AB
GIVEN BY CHANEL

While trends of the 1970s sparked renewed interest in crochet, it is not a technique often associated with haute couture. Just as years earlier Chanel had introduced more humble textiles such as jerseys and tweeds to her collections, her adoption of another textile foreign to the world of couture – crochet – reveals once again her tendency to subvert the accepted codes. Frequently used to make blankets, bags and simple, casual garments in multiple colours, crocheting was considered more of a domestic activity. Here, Chanel brought sophistication to the artisanal technique. The powder pink wool is mixed with iridescent Lurex, and the complex stitches give an openwork effect specific to crochet, producing a delicate and refined material suitable for a formal evening outfit. The necklace, sewn around the neckline of the sweater, comprises faceted rock-crystal pendants in gilt-metal settings, underlining the importance of jewellery to the Chanel look. Evoking fine jewellery, Chanel plays with her own codes by naturally integrating the adornment into the garment, creating an attractive trompe-l'oeil effect. **VB**

By the end of the 1960s, Chanel was firmly known, once again, for her suits, yet she continued to produce innovative eveningwear, often drawing on the techniques and styles of her earlier years. This dress with its deft handling of chiffon, shirred close to the bodice then flowing out at the skirt, recalls the designer's lightweight evening dresses of the 1930s but is instantly brought up to date by the startlingly bright and playful rainbow colourway and the free-flowing chiffon drape of the voluminous neck scarf. **OC**

72. DRESS

SPRING/SUMMER 1968
SILK CHIFFON
PATRIMOINE DE CHANEL, PARIS:
HC.PE.1968.7

To take a style that was the ultimate in quotidian dressing and transform it into an easy yet elegant proposition for formal wear was typical of Chanel's ethos. The shirt dress as ballgown was a modern idea that appealed to the couturière and a style to which she returned throughout her career (see no.47). It demonstrates Chanel's consistency of approach to the last, harking back to the early 1930s when she introduced humble cotton as an option for eveningwear (see no.37), while simultaneously continuing to innovate and evolve. The cut of this dress – the fitted bodice with wide pointed lapels resting on the shoulders and casually tied sash belt – situates it firmly in the 1970s. Chanel's organdie cotton dresses, often in white, were frequently associated with a younger clientele. Here, the inclusion of a playful daisy pattern woven into the fabric gives a youthful look. This shirt dress was part of the finale of Chanel's final collection, presented posthumously in January 1971, one of the three white evening dresses that closed the show.[62] **OC**

73. DRESS
SPRING/SUMMER 1971
COTTON ORGANDIE
PATRIMOINE DE CHANEL, PARIS:
HC.PE.1971.20

Fig. 100 Look No.78 from Gabrielle Chanel's last collection, Spring/Summer 1971, shown posthumously. Modelled by Marilou Cherqui. Patrimoine de CHANEL, Paris

On 2 December 1978, seven years after her death, Christie's auction house in London organized a sale of Chanel's garments, compiled by her former assistant of 14 years, Lilou Marquand. The sale was not without controversy. Some close to the designer felt it was out of keeping with what she would have wished; others questioned the authenticity of the provenance of the items: the items were definitely by Chanel but did they all belong to Gabrielle Chanel? Yet, the designer's legendary status ensured there was much interest and a great attendance at the event. Chanel was inextricably linked with the classic black-and-white colour palette and it was this black suit with matching boater-style hat that featured on the cover of the auction catalogue. The suit, Look 21 from the Autumn/Winter 1969 collection, consists of a sleeveless dress and longline jacket, originally worn with a white roll-collar blouse, giving it the air of a religious habit. Listed as Lot 93, it was purchased by the V&A for £1430. As with each of the garments sold at the auction it has a special label stitched inside the lining recording the sale. No pictures exist of Chanel wearing this suit, so it is difficult to confirm or deny its provenance. Regardless of this fact, it remains a timeless ensemble, as relevant and wearable today as it was when first created over 50 years ago, a perfect legacy of the strength of Chanel's design credo. Journalist Prudence Glynn commented at the time: 'It is impossible to chart pictorially the evolution of Chanel as a designer because she did not evolve. Rather fashion evolved round her. She created a look which was overwhelmingly successful when it was launched and which has left in-erradicable traces in fashion.'[63] **OC**

74. SUIT

AUTUMN/WINTER 1969
WORSTED WOOL CREPE;
REPRODUCTION COLLAR AND CUFFS
V&A: T.22-1979

Fig. 101 Model Maija Porkka poses on the mirrored staircase in the Chanel salon, wearing a black wool suit, Look No.21, from the Autumn/Winter 1969 collection. Patrimoine de CHANEL, Paris

INTRODUCTION

1 See Select Bibliography.
2 Morand 2008, p.34.
3 Charles-Roux 1989, p.111.
4 Ibid., pl.21.
5 Sophie Grossiord, 'The Early Days of the "Artist of the Rue Cambon"', in Arzalluz and Belloir 2020, pp.15–19.
6 Georges Goursat, *Tangoville sur Mer* (Paris 1913).
7 Charles-Roux 1989, p.134.
8 'Fashion: Chanel is Master of Her Art, and Her Art Resides in Jersey', American *Vogue* (1 November 1916), p.65.
9 Charles-Roux 1989, p.134.
10 'Features: Deauville Before the War', American *Vogue* (1 September 1914), p.31.
11 Chanel also combined silk jersey with cotton jersey, see Jeanne Ramon Fernandez, 'Exponents of the Salons of Chanel', American *Vogue* (1 April 1918), p.43.
12 'What Fashionable Folk Are Wearing at Deauville', *The New York Times* (21 September 1913), p.14.
13 de la Haye 2011, p.20.
14 'Features: Deauville Before the War', American *Vogue* (1 September 1914), p.27.
15 'Fashion: Chanel is Master of Her Art, and Her Art Resides in Jersey', American *Vogue* (1 November 1916), p.65.
16 'Informal Jersey Suits Replace Elegant Styles of Yore', *New York Herald*, European edition (4 June 1916), p.2.
17 Jeanne Ramon Fernandez, 'Fashion: Paris Sets Forth the Mode of 1919', American *Vogue* (1 April 1919), p.122.
18 Haedrich 1972, p.119.
19 Ibid.
20 'Fashion: The Debut of the Winter Mode', American *Vogue* (1 October 1926), p.69.
21 Morand 2008, p.81.
22 Ibid.
23 'Three Points of View from Paris', American *Vogue* (1 May 1922), p.39. Also confirmed by the employees registrar in the Chanel archives.
24 Charles-Roux 1989, p.181.
25 Julian Blanshard, 'New Ideas on Advanced Perfumery', *Indianapolis Times* (16 March 1931), p.6.
26 Mazzeo 2011, p.67.
27 Phillida, 'Secrecy Scents', *Daily Mirror* (7 December 1925), p.18.
28 Madsen 1990, pp.200–1.
29 Lodwick 2015, pp.164–5.
30 Madsen 1990, pp.120, 160.
31 Madame X, 'A Woman's Letter', *The Graphic* (6 October 1928), p.22.
32 Field 1983, p.201.
33 'Ina Claire Selects the Newest Chanel Sports Frocks in Tweed and Velveteen', American *Vogue* (15 November 1924), p.46.
34 'Scotch Tweed: The Latest Godchild of the French Couturiers', American *Vogue* (15 October 1927), p.104.
35 Galante 1972, p.121.
36 Genty 2019, p.138.
37 Ibid., p.140.
38 McFadyean/6/3, London School of Economics Archives.
39 A première is the French term for the head of an atelier, or workroom.
40 'Chanel Opens her London House', *Vogue* (June 1927), p.49.
41 'Advertisement: Beautiful CLOTHES', *Lemington Spa Courier* (6 May 1927), p.5.
42 'Textiles Scheme: Yorkshire Co-operation with Paris House', *Yorkshire Post and Leeds Intelligencer* (6 April 1932), p.10.
43 Ibid.
44 'French Chic and British Material: Nottingham Firms Co-operate with Paris', *Nottingham Journal* (7 May 1932), p.7.
45 'Society Girls as Mannequins: Showing New British Fashions', *Gloucester Journal* (7 May 1932), p.9.
46 'How To Wear British: Paris Creator Shows Us the Way', *Birmingham Daily Gazette* (6 May 1932), p.8.
47 McFadyean/6/3, London School of Economics Archives.
48 'Kirkheaton Firm and Paris Fashions', *Huddersfield and Holmfirth Examiner* (25 February 1933), p.8.
49 'French-Yorkshire Fabrics', *Leeds Mercury* (3 October 1933), p.8.
50 'Kirkheaton Firm in New Fabric Company', *Leeds Mercury* (21 February 1933), p.5.
51 Carlisle Archives DB110/181, Swatchbook–1887–1937, newspaper cutting dated 24 February 1933.
52 'Duchess Visits White City: Purchase in Textile Section', *Yorkshire Post and Leeds Intelligencer* (21 February 1933), p.4.
53 For example, see *L'Officiel* (October 1949), p.67.
54 'Designer Finds Beauty Based on Simplicity and Workmanship', *Washington Star* (15 March 1931), p.13.
55 Beaton 1954, p.164.
56 Séguret 1990, p.137.
57 Mauriès 2014, p.29.
58 Mabel Howard, 'Women's Ways', *The Sketch* (19 October 1927), p.163.
59 Mauriès 1993, p.32.
60 Charles-Roux 1989, p.268.
61 'New Fashion Queen', *Daily Herald* (20 January 1931), p.1.
62 *The Bioscope* (8 April 1931), p.29.
63 Picardie 2010, p.211.
64 'We Nominate for the Hall of Fame', *Vanity Fair* (June 1931), p.66.
65 Chaney 2011, p.261.
66 de la Haye 2011, p.67.
67 Janet Flanner, 'Paris Letter', *New Yorker* (3 December 1932), p.34.
68 'Bijoux de Diamants', French *Vogue* (1 January 1933), p.25.
69 Janet Flanner, 'Paris Letter', *New Yorker* (3 December 1932), p.34.
70 Sylvia Lyon, 'Changes and Charms in Paris', *The Bystander* (23 April 1930), p.170.
71 Young 2019, p.147.
72 Vreeland 1984, pp.95, 129.
73 Ballard 1960, p.55.
74 Ibid., p.137.
75 'Fashion: Out of the Paris Openings a New Breath of Life', American *Vogue* (1 March 1939), p.52.
76 'Fashion World: Blouse and Skirt – for Evening Wear', *Manchester Evening News* (21 March 1939), p.3.
77 'Fashion: Out of the Paris Openings a New Breath of Life', American *Vogue* (1 March 1939), p.52.
78 Fiemeyer 2011, p.169.
79 Ibid.
80 Fiemeyer 2016, p.135.
81 World Committee for the Victims of German Fascism, *The Brown Network: The Activities of the Nazis in Foreign Countries*, trans. Clement Greenberg, New York 1936, p.94.
82 Z/6762 Greffe 5559, Archives Nationale, Paris, p.597.
83 Fiemeyer 2016, pp.184–5.
84 Archives Nationales, Paris: CGQJ AJ–38–2725; Bruno Abescat and Yves Stavridès, 'Le retour du Mexicain, Derrière l'empire Chanel…La fabuleuse histoire des Wertheimer', *l'Express*

(17 July 2005), https://www.lexpress.fr/economie/3-le-retour-du-mexicain_485150.html (accessed 13 February 2023).

85 BA1990/5455, Archives de la Préfecture de Police, Paris. Investigations after the war found no evidence of a dossier containing information supplied by Chanel, see Z/6762 Greffe 5559, Archives Nationale, Paris, p.620.

86 Documents in the French National Archives report that Chanel previously travelled to Spain in August 1941 with Baron Louis de Vaufreland (see Z/6762 Greffe, Archives Nationale, p.632), who Chanel later claimed was responsible for the release of her nephew (see Z/6762 Greffe, Archives Nationale, pp.341–4). While there, she had dinner with British diplomat, Brian Wallace (see Vaughan 2012, pp.162–4). In 1948 Chanel was called as a witness in the trial of de Vaufreland, who was charged with cooperation with the enemy.

87 Doerries 2003, p.108.

88 Ibid., p.109. Schellenberg also reported that Chanel and Dincklage travelled to Berlin to meet with him in April 1944.

89 Bruno Abescat and Yves Stavridès, 'Le retour du Mexicain, Derrière l'empire Chanel…La fabuleuse histoire des Wertheimer', l'Express (17 July 2005), https://www.lexpress.fr/economie/3-le-retour-du-mexicain_485150.html (accessed 13 February 2023).

90 'Parfums Chanel Sued by Designer', The New York Times (3 June 1946), p.28.

91 Chaney 2011, p.349. 'Mlle. Chanel, Famous Clothes Designer, Puts Her Special Imprint on these Rooms', American Vogue (15 August 1953), pp.112–13.

92 Madsen 1990, p.285.

93 '"Coco" Chanel, Famed Stylist of 20s, Will Reopen Salon', Washington Evening Star (16 December 1953), p.A-21.

94 'Chanel Designs Again', American Vogue (15 February 1954), pp.83–5.

95 Elizabeth Fairall, 'Paris Letter', Washington Evening Star (10 February 1954), p.B-6.

96 Marjorie Proops, 'Come Back', Daily Herald (18 February 1954), p.6; Geoffrey Hoare, 'But Can Mlle Do It Again?', Daily London News (6 February 1954), p.2.

97 Jean Wiseman, 'Watch Out, M. Dior', Aberdeen Evening Express (7 May 1954), p.4.

98 'Paris Collections: One Easy Lesson', American Vogue (1 March 1954), pp.101–2.

99 'Party News Coming from Paris', American Vogue (1 November 1954), p.99.

100 'Coco Chanel Shows New Dress Collection', Washington Evening Star (7 October 1954), p.B-4.

101 Rosamond Bernier, 'Chanel', British Vogue (February 1954), p.73.

102 de la Haye 2011, p.60.

103 'Lightweight Wool for Between the Seasons', Tatler (8 May 1957), p.37.

104 Rosamond Bernier, 'Chanel', British Vogue (February 1954), p.73.

105 Kent 1980.

106 Jean Denys, 'Chanel aujourd'hui', French Elle (17 November 1958), pp.46–61; 'C'est etre merveilleuse avec le petit tailleur de Chanel', French Elle, (4 December 1959), pp.102–7.

107 Ailsa Garland, 'Yes, Dior's "Heir" is Good – But Not Yet Great', Daily Mirror (30 January 1959), p.7.

108 Jill Bateman, 'For the Spring Buy a Suit', Bognor Regis Observer (6 February 1959), p.6.

109 Morand 2008, p.154.

110 'CHANEL. Triumphant – A Collection More Dashing than Ever', American Vogue (15 September 1964), p.115.

111 Mauriès 2014, p.37.

112 Kate Betts, 'Vogue's View: Foot Soldier', American Vogue (1 November 1992), p.120.

113 'Chanel To Be Presented 1957 Fashion Award', Washington Evening Star (19 August 1957), p.B-4.

114 Alison Adburgham, 'Coco Chanel's Stylish Exit', The Guardian (26 January 1971), https://www.theguardian.com/fashion/2022/jan/26/coco-chanel-stylish-exit-archive-1971 (accessed 28 November 2022).

115 Prudence Glynn, 'Chanel the Now and Future Look', The Times (27 January 1971), p.9.

116 Ibid.

117 Alison Adburgham, 'Coco Chanel's Stylish Exit', The Guardian (26 January 1971), https://www.theguardian.com/fashion/2022/jan/26/coco-chanel-stylish-exit-archive-1971 (accessed 28 November 2022).

GALLERY

1 Ralph Breed, 'Paris Suggests These New Silhouettes', American Vogue (1 February 1918), p.42.

2 'The New Parisienne, Hoopless and in Furs', American Vogue (15 July 1916), p.38.

3 'C'est La Victoire!', American Vogue (1 February 1919), p.35.

4 Ibid.

5 'Paris Weather Vanes are Set for Change of Mode', American Vogue (1 September 1919), pp.36–7.

6 Ibid.

7 Bibliothèque nationale de France, Dept Estampes et Photographie, EI-13(2599), Agence Meurisse, Photograph 73069, 29 June 1919.

8 'Paris Dines and Dances and Awaits the Openings', American Vogue (15 March 1919), p.35.

9 'Fashion: Three Points of View from Paris', American Vogue (1 May 1921), p.124.

10 Vassiliev 2000, p.163.

11 'New Models from Cheruit and Chanel', American Vogue (1 March 1922), p.56. The accompanying illustration also appeared in the French edition in April.

12 Sokolova 1960, p.221.

13 'En L'Été de 1926', French Vogue (1 June 1926), p.16.

14 'Paris Fashions', The Times (4 March 1929), p.19.

15 Grace Duggan officially made her debut in the season of 1927, but her mother held the first ball to celebrate her society 'coming out' in December 1926.

16 E.W. Boulter, 'What Paris is Going to Wear', Bystander (15 September 1926), p.42.

17 Candida, 'Frills and Frivolities', The Graphic (19 June 1926), p.32.

18 'A Portfolio of the New York Evening Mode', American Vogue (1 November 1926), p.71.

19 'Shaded Fringe is Favoured in Paris', Belington Progressive (10 March 1927), p.2.

20 Anita Leslie, The Gilt and the Gingerbread (London 1981), p.132.

21 'Fashionable Accessories for the London Season', The Illustrated London News (21 April 1928), p.42.

22 'Les Caprices de la Mode', Paris-Midi (5 September 1927), p.8.

23 W.B., 'Chic', Britannia and Eve (26 October 1928), p.75.

24 'A Guide to Chic for the Golfer', American Vogue (15 June 1926), p.82.

25 'Tweed is an Essential of the Smart New Wardrobe', American Vogue (1 November 1926), pp.76–7.

26 'The Death of Minoru, Lady Foley', Kensington News and West London Times (26 April 1968), p.10.

27 'The Parisienne Seeks Individuality in Dress', The New York Times (13 December 1936), p.102.

28 'Chanel', French Vogue (1 April 1926), p.64.

29 'Coudurier, Fructus & Drescher', French Vogue (1 February 1929), p.27.

30 Jean Burnup, 'Personally Speaking', Britannia and Eve (1 April 1938), p.56.

31 'Autumn Modes', Bexhill-on-Sea Observer (7 October 1933), p.2.

32 'Fashion: Paris Puts Lace on a Feminine Mode', American Vogue (10 November 1930), p.114.

33 Gabrielle Chanel, 'Dentelle', L'Illustration (29 April 1939), p.8.

34 'Paris Fashions', The Times (15 August 1932), p.13.

35 'Paris Fashions', The Times (27 August 1934), p.13.

36 Paris Interprets Summer Chic in New Cottons', The New York Times (26 April 1931), p.13.

37 'Seaside Dresses', Liverpool Daily Post (5 June 1933), p.6.

38 'Organdie', Britannia and Eve (1 June 1933), p.70.

39 Lois Long, 'On and Off the Avenue: Feminine Fashions', New Yorker (22 March 1930), p.70.

40 'Designer Finds Beauty Based on Simplicity and Workmanship', Washington Sunday Star (15 March 1931), p.15.

41 'The Parisienne Seeks Individuality in Dress', New York Times (13 December 1936), p.102.

42 'Mid Season Paris Fashions', The Times (15 November 1937), p.19.

43 Ibid.

44 'Paris Shows 1937–38, Evening Gowns in Round Figures', The New York Times (12 September 1937), p.6.

45 'A New Gilet Dress is Shown by Rouff', The New York Times (4 February 1939), p.17.

46 'Coco Chanel Shows New Dress Collection', Washington Evening Star (7 October 1954), p.B-4.

47 'Chanel News: Complete Evening Coverage', American Vogue (1 December 1954), p.132.

48 'Fashion: Paris News A to Z', American Vogue (1 March 1955), p.99.

49 Hazel Hackett, 'These Paris Styles Are So Easy to Wear', Belfast Telegraph (19 September 1956), p.3.

50 Charles Castle, Model Girl (New York 1977), p.44.

51 'The Paris Idea', British Vogue, May 1964, p.78.

52 Mauriès 2014, p.37.

53 Ibid., p.50.

54 Haedrich 1972, p.184.

55 Mauriès 2014, p.21.

56 Joseph Barry, 'Portrait of Chanel No.1', The New York Times (23 August 1964), p.110.

57 'Fashion: Chanel, the Great Little Tweed Suits… Smaller, Narrower', American Vogue (15 March 1966), p.90.

58 'Index', American Vogue (1 October 1961), p.3.

59 Nathalie Pernikoff, 'A Hat Trick of Hits', Birmingham Daily Post (30 July 1964), p.7.

60 'Fashion: Forecast 1969', American Vogue (1 January 1969), p.94.

61 'Chanel – Her Famous New Dinner Pyjamas', American Vogue (15 November 1965), p.116.

62 'Coco Is Missed', The New York Times (27 January 1971), p.42.

63 Prudence Glynn, 'Chanel: Public Fame and Private Enigma', The Times (12 January 1971), p.7.

SELECT BIBLIOGRAPHY

Miren Arzalluz and Véronique Belloir (eds), *Gabrielle Chanel. Fashion Manifesto* (Paris 2020)

Bettina Ballard, *In My Fashion* (New York 1960)

Cecil Beaton, *The Glass of Fashion* (London 1954)

Lisa Chaney, *Coco Chanel: An Intimate Life* (New York 2011)

Edmonde Charles-Roux, *Chanel* (1974), trans. Nancy Amphoux (London 1989)

Amy de la Haye, *Chanel: Couture and Industry* (London 2011)

Reinhard R. Doerries, *Hitler's Last Chief of Foreign Intelligence: Allied Interrogations of Walter Schellenberg* (London and Portland 2003)

Leslie Field, *Bendor: The Golden Duke of Westminster* (London 1983)

Isabelle Fiemeyer, *Chanel intime* (Paris 2011)

Isabelle Fiemeyer, *Chanel: The Enigma* (Paris 2016)

Pierre Galante, *Les Années Chanel* (Paris 1972)

Marika Genty, 'Weaving Words', *Iliazd Colloquium*, 6–7 June (Paris 2019), pp.136–49

Marcel Haedrich, *Coco Chanel: Her Life Her Secrets* (New York 1972)

Malhia Kent, *La Pharaonne* (Paris 1980)

Keith Lodwick, 'Diaghilev and Chanel', in Jane Pritchard (ed.), *Diaghilev and the Golden Age of the Ballets Russes 1909–1929*, exh. cat., V&A (London 2015), pp.164–5

Axel Madsen, *Chanel: A Woman of Her Own* (New York 1990)

Patrick Mauriès, *Jewelry by CHANEL* (London 1993)

Patrick Mauriès, *Maison Goossens: Haute Couture Jewelry* (London 2014)

Tilar J. Mazzeo, *The Secret of Chanel N°5* (New York 2011)

Paul Morand, *The Allure of Chanel* (1976), trans. Euan Cameron (London 2008)

Justine Picardie, *Coco Chanel: The Legend and the Life* (London 2010)

Olivier Séguret, *Haute Couture: Tradesmen's Entrance* (Paris 1990)

Lydia Sokolova, *Dancing for Diaghilev* (London 1960)

Maria Spitz (ed.), *The Chanel Legend* (Mettingen 2013)

Alexandre Vassiliev, *Beauty in Exile*, trans. Antonia W. Bouis and Anya Kucharev (New York 2000)

Hal Vaughan, *Sleeping with the Enemy: Coco Chanel's Secret War* (New York 2012)

Diana Vreeland, *D.V.* (New York 1984)

World Committee for the Victims of German Fascism, *The Brown Network: The Activities of the Nazis in Foreign Countries*, trans. Clement Greenberg (New York 1936)

Caroline Young, *Living with Coco Chanel: The Homes and Landscapes that Shaped the Designer* (London 2019)

PICTURE CREDITS

ACKNOWLEDGEMENTS

We are hugely grateful to the many colleagues throughout the V&A who have provided support, expertise and time to make this project possible. A special thank you to Rachael Lee and Francis Hartog for all their expertise and work conserving and mounting the garments for this publication and the exhibition. Thank you to Tom Windross, Coralie Hepburn and Kirstin Beattie for guiding this process and for their work on the book, to the designer Daniela Rocha, and to Emma Woodiwiss, Susannah Priede, Andrew Tullis and Lucy Macmillan. Particular thanks go to Jacques Schuhmacher for giving his time and expertise, to Evgeniya Ravtsova for delving into archives, and to Jo Norman. Thank you to all of our colleagues in the Performance, Furniture, Textiles and Fashion department, especially Christopher Wilk, Sonnet Stanfill, Jane Pritchard and Kate Bailey. Many thanks to Sabrina Offord, Clare Phillips, Lydia Caston, Ruth Hibbard and Katrina Redman for helping us access and examine Chanel objects across the museum's collection. We are grateful to Kira Zumkley and the V&A Photography and Digitization team for the V&A images in this publication. Very special thanks to Daniel Slater, Olivia Oldroyd, Harriet Seabourne, Sarah Jameson, Lyndsey Snook, Roo Gunzi and Fiona Ibbetson for their incredible work making this project happen.

This exhibition and accompanying publication were made possible by the generosity and cooperation of Hélène Fulgence and the team at Patrimoine de CHANEL. Thank you to Odile Prémel, Marika Genty, Cécile Goddet Dirles, Julie Deydier, Marie Hamelin Dufief, Sarah Piettre and Stephane Bedhome for welcoming us at the archive and sharing their incredible expertise about the objects and history of Chanel. Thank you to Laura Draghici-Foulon for her input and work in making this publication possible, and to Laurène Flinois and Chloé Petel.

Thank you to Miren Arzalluz and the team at the Palais Galliera, Véronique Belloir and Anais Quinsat, for their collegiality and generous contributions throughout this project.

Special thanks to Spencer Bailey and the team at Derby Museums who made it possible to feature two of the collections' Chanel dresses in this publication, and to all the collections, individuals and institutions who generously lent their objects to the exhibition. For supporting and facilitating our research, we would also like to thank Amy de la Haye, Justine Picardie, Katy Conover, Katherine Howells, Duncan Walker and John Wooding.

We are grateful to Nicholas Alan Cope for creating such striking images for this publication. Thanks also go to Vidhya Rassou and the team at Kitten Production for staging the shoot at the V&A and the Patrimoine de CHANEL; to Sylvain Cabouat, Rémi Bassemon, Denis Shklovsky and the rest of the shoot team; and to the team at The Post Office, who all made possible the beautiful images included here.

INDEX